The
Grand
Canyon

text by

Letitia Burns O'Connor

photography by

Tom Bean

John Blaustein

Michael Collier

D.T. DeDomenico

Dana Levy

David Muench

Greg Probst

John Running

Paul Vucetich

HUGH LAUTER LEVIN ASSOCIATES, INC.

Distributed by Macmillan Publishing Company, New York

The Grand Canyon was produced for Hugh Lauter Levin Associates, Inc.
by Perpetua Press, Los Angeles

Printed in Hong Kong

ISBN: 0-88363-792-8

Tom Bean: front cover, 9, 37, 39, 42, 43, 46-48, 53 center, 54, 55, 56 top, 57, 60 bottom left, 62 top right, 63 top right, 78 top right, 82, 86, 90 top, 91, 95 left, 96 left, 102 top, 104 right, 123 top left, 126.

John Blaustein: 11, 98 left and right, 99, 100 top, 101, 107, 109 right, 112 left and right, 114-115, 118 right, 122 right, 123 bottom left, 124 bottom center, 125 top right, 128.

Michael Collier: 14, 36 right, 53 left center, 66 left and right, 67, 88, 106

D. T. De Domenico: 7, 36 left, 62 top left, 74 bottom, 90 bottom, 92 top and bottom, 100 bottom, 111 right, 118 left, 124 center,

Dana Levy: 2-4, 49, 50, 51 right, 69-70, 74 top, 84-85, 92-93, 94

David Muench: back cover, 1, 10, 40 right, 41 left, 45, 51 left, 52 left, 58, 59 right, 73, 77, 79, 80, 83, 87, 89, 97 left, 113, 117 left, 119 left, 127;
Marc Muench: 117 right

Greg Probst: 12, 13, 44, 68, 72 left and right, 81, 95 top and bottom right, 116, 121

John Running: 6, 60 bottom right, 61 bottom left, 62 bottom right, 63 left, 103 top left, 104 left, 105, 108 left, 109 left, 111 left, 122 bottom center, 124 left, 125 center bottom, 125 left

Paul Vucetich: 8, 38, 53 top center, 56 bottom, 59 left top and bottom, 60 top, 61 six photos, 62 lower left, 76 left, 78 left, 78 bottom right, 96 right, 97 right, 102, 103, 119 right, 120 left and right, 122 bottom left, 123 bottom center, 123 top right

COVER: A rainbow pierces a golden sunset over Grand Canyon, viewed from Yaki Point.

BACK COVER: Moisture-laden atmosphere and back lighting create special effects in the canyon at dusk.

PAGE 1: Afternoon light casts strong shadows that highlight a geological cross section from Point Imperial on the North Rim. Mount Hayden is the pyramidal shape in the foreground.

PAGE 2–4: Panorama from Lipan Point.

PAGE 6: Cactus frame a view of the Colorado River from Eminence Break in Marble Canyon.

PAGE 7: Sunset view of the palisades along the Colorado from the Desert View overlook.

Rain at sunset over Oza Butte, looking south from Grand
Canyon Lodge, North Rim

OPPOSITE

The setting sun colors canyon walls viewed from the South
Kaibab Trail, a popular hiking route.

Unkar Creek Rapids forms a reverse curve of the Colorado River as it cuts through striated red-and-white layers of the Grand Canyon Series. This view from Lipan Point on the South Rim is probably that seen in 1540 by Spanish explorer Garcia Lopez de Cardenas, who was led to the canyon rim, reportedly at this location, by Hopi guides.

Opposite

Rough pink cliffs dwarf a boat on the Colorado.

"There are cliffs and ledges of rock—not such ledges as you may have seen where the quarryman splits his blocks, but ledges from which the gods might quarry mountains...and not such cliffs as you may have seen where the swallow builds its nest, but cliffs where the soaring eagle is lost to view ere he reaches the summit. Wherever we look there is but a wilderness of rocks; deep gorges, where the rivers are lost below the cliffs; towers and pinnacles and ten thousand strangely carved forms in every direction; and beyond them, mountains blending with the clouds."

JOHN WESLEY POWELL, *Exploration of the Colorado River of the West and its Tributaries*, 1875

Boulder dominates view into canyon from Yaki Point.

OPPOSITE

Light snow highlights canyon forms in another view from Yaki Point. O'Neill Butte, in the foreground, and the complex structure of Wotans Throne dominate the composition.

CANYON PERSPECTIVES

by Letitia Burns O'Connor

THE GRAND CANYON, which occupies most of northwestern Arizona, extends from Lees Ferry near the Utah border to Lake Mead on the Nevada border in the west. In 1919 the Grand Canyon became a National Park, and today it encompasses 1,900 square miles. In 1979 it was named a World Heritage Site, recognized as an ecosystem unique in the world with a cultural value equivalent to the Olympic Rain Forest, Chartres cathedral, and the Egyptian pyramids, which have also been so designated.

One mile beneath the canyon rim, the Colorado River meanders 277 miles within the park, which many consider the crown jewel of America's natural treasures. The average distance between the north and south rims of the canyon is ten miles, a chasm filled with red, gray, and ochre cliffs that descend in gigantic stepped terraces and climb in towers, buttes, and mesas of mountainous proportions. Named not for the state but with a Spanish word meaning "red colored," the Colorado River courses 1,400 miles from the midwest to the Gulf of California.

The Colorado River runs roughly north-south through Marble Canyon and for the first seventy miles within the park, then turns west after the confluence of the Little Colorado River for the rest of its looping course. The river lies much closer to the South Rim, which is relatively straight with steep short canyons dropping to the river. On the South Rim elevations vary from 6,000 to 7,500 feet; they are up to 2,000 feet higher on the North. The prevailing slope of the land is from the North Rim to the river, producing a broad drainage north of the river characterized by deep tributary canyons as much as fifteen miles long. The North Rim thus has a very irregular shape, which includes promontories—for example, at Point Sublime and Cape Royal—that extend several miles into the canyon and afford panoramic vistas. The Kaibab Forest and alpine meadows bright with wildflowers characterize the scenery away from the North Rim, which receives only 10 percent of the total visitors to the Grand Canyon because of its more isolated approach and shorter season (snow makes North Rim roads impassable from late October to May).

The different altitudes within the canyon, as well as the four distinct seasons that characterize this part of the Southwest, produce a varied climatic range: from desert environments with less than ten inches of rain annually on the canyon floor, below 2,000 feet, to scrub/piñon/juniper woodlands (called the Upper Sonoran Zone) that mark the 2,000 to 7,000-foot elevations, which includes both rims of the canyon. The

Ponderosa pine forests on both rims identify another climatic zone, typically found between 6,500 and 7,500 feet, as here. The North Rim, with elevations above 8,000 feet and 30 inches of precipitation annually, hosts the Canadian Zone, which is marked by subalpine forests of spruce and aspen.

Geology and the Formation of the Grand Canyon

CARVED BY THE COLORADO RIVER, its tributaries, and other forces of erosion, the formations that fill this great gorge reveal the ancient geological substratum of the Earth's crust. During a period of four to six million years, the Grand Canyon has been sculpted through one mile of solid rock by the Colorado River. In 1901 John Muir described the topographical orientation of the canyon, which is one of its most distinctive

ABOVE
Runoff, caused by violent storms, is one of the main forces of erosion that has sculpted the Grand Canyon. John Blaustein, who was a boatman on river trips when he shot this view, recalls dodging showers of debris and rocks—some as large as boulders—following such rain storms. Photograph by John Blaustein.

LEFT
Aerial view of a fire, ignited by lightening, on Powell Plateau, 1990. Photograph by Greg Probst.

CENTER
Debris carried to the mouth of the side canyons forms many of the rapids along the Colorado. Photograph by John Blaustein.

<Opposite
Aerial view of the northeast corner of Grand Canyon National Park. The Colorado River cuts through the Echo Cliffs Monocline at Lees Ferry, Arizona, which is visible in the bottom right.

Timothy O'Sullivan, *Wall in the Grand Cañon, Colorado River*, 1871. Courtesy of Amon Carter Museum, Fort Worth.

Right

Timothy O'Sullivan, *Looking Across the Colorado River to the Mouth of Paria Creek*, 1873. Courtesy of Amon Carter Museum, Fort Worth.

features: "It is abruptly countersunk in the forest plateau, so that you see nothing of it until you are suddenly stopped on its brink with its immeasurable wealth of divinely colored and sculptured buildings before and beneath you."

Anyone who looks over the rim develops a sudden interest in geology. Sedimentary, igneous, and metamorphic rocks can easily be distinguished in the multicolored layers of the canyon. The geologic history of the area encompasses a rock strata at the canyon base that is about two billion years old. The human concept of time is confounded by the dizzying numbers of geologic time. The National Park Rangers try to give visitors an understanding of the canyon and its formation by explaining such forces as uplift and the various forms of erosion that created this extraordinary space.

During the last four million years, water has shaped the canyon's formations, revealing two billion years of geologic activity. The canyon formations of Redwall Limestone—located about halfway between the rim and the river—and several layers below it, including Muav Limestone and Bright Angel Shale, reveal that the land that is now a desert was submerged beneath an ocean 500 million years ago. In the Redwall Limestone, which characteristically weathers into vertical cliffs more than 500 feet high, and the strata below it are numerous marine fossils, animals stranded when the shallow sea became a swampish plain 300 million years ago. Sixty-five million years ago the uplift of the Colorado Plateau, which geologists attribute to extraordinary forces deep within the earth's crust, positioned the area for sculpting by deep watercourses.

The earliest rock layer in the canyon dates from the Early Precambrian period 1.7 to 2 billion years ago and forms the dark, steep walls along the Colorado River gorge. The three types of schist and granite within this layer shared a volcanic origin but have been further transformed by heat and pressure. This layer's structure includes "marked vertical ridges, called "foliation," which contrast with the horizontal layerings elsewhere in the canyon formations. The most recent rock layer in the canyon is composed of grey and creamy Kaibab and Toroweap limestone, which is 250 million years old.[1]

Erosion continues to sculpt the canyon landscape in areas no longer scoured by the river, its particular effect determined by such factors as the amount of precipitation and ambient temperatures. For example, water seeps through cracks and porous rock, freezing, then sending torrents of stone crashing down with the spring melt, altering the canyon's formations with a phenomenon called "weathering." Or, heavy rain carries massive amounts of dirt and smaller rocks down to the river, where it becomes the sediment that gives the Colorado its reddish-brown color, a process geologists call "transport." Such processes, including the force of tributary streams and rivers, have produced the outward expansion of the canyon from the crevice carved by the Colorado itself.

Human Encounters with the Canyon

The HUMAN HISTORY of the area extends 5,000 years to Native American exploration and habitation of the canyon. By A.D. 500 the Anasazi, Pueblo, and Cohonina Indians settled on the canyon floor, eventually establishing more than 1,000 sites, many still identified today by pictographs and cave paintings. By A.D. 1300 all of the groups had abandoned permanent residence in the canyon. Whether driven out by tribes new to the area or by population too great for the available resources of an arid land, by the end of the Great Drought of 1276–1299, Native Americans no longer lived there. The Grand Canyon continued to play a central role in the mythology and spiritual life of Native peoples. According to historian J. Donald Hughes, the Havasupai, whose ancestors the Cerbat Indians led a post-Drought migration into the western part of the canyon, called the canyon "Wikatata, or Rough Rim, and to the Hopi it is the place of emergence from and descent into the underworld. The Paiutes knew of water 'deep down in the earth.'"[2] Photographer Jack Hillers documented the life of some Native peoples of the canyon, photographing the Kaibab Paiute Indians, who lived part of the year near Kanab, Utah, and the Hopi villages. The reservations of the Hualapai, Havasupai, and Navajo now include parts of canyon lands.

Today a torrent of visitors from around the world is drawn to experience not only this planet's most outstanding geological exhibit but a spectacle of nature of such grand proportions that it overwhelms human sensory perceptions. Early explorers had mixed reactions. Eighty years before the Pilgrims landed at Plymouth Rock, Spanish conquistadores had been led to the edge of the Grand Canyon by Indian guides. In 1540 a baffled Garcia Lopez de Cardenas, traveling with a contingent of men from Coronado's expedition to locate the Seven Cities of Cibola, estimated the size of the river he saw below to be less than ten feet wide.

For fifty years from circa 1840, as the United States pursued its "manifest destiny" to stretch from the Atlantic to the Pacific, surveyors, engineers, and scientists traveled through the exotic and barren western landscape plotting its economic development. When these lands became U.S. territory in 1848, in a treaty settling the Mexican War, they were largely uncharted and almost inaccessible.

The magnificent Grand Canyon of the Colorado River was not surveyed until the disruption of the Civil War ended, when Major John Wesley Powell (1834-

1902) led a series of expeditions to study its geology, beginning in 1869. He remained at the forefront of scientific exploration of the canyon for the next twenty years and his became the most important name in the human history of the Grand Canyon.

The first Powell expedition, which left Green River Station, Wyoming, in May 1869, was poorly funded, and so no photographer or illustrator was included in the group. One of the expedition's four boats, which carried most of their food, capsized in the Canyon of Lodore, forcing the party to proceed with the greatest speed to outlast the meager rations that remained. Circumstances thus prevented Powell from acquiring the data necessary to plot the course of the river, but he had learned methods of surviving on the roughest water in the United States that would ensure the scientific success of a later mission.

Powell set off from the same location two years later, but he intended to spend about eighteen months rather than the hurried one hundred days of the first expedition. His boats had been redesigned and arrangements made to resupply the party with provisions deposited at several points along their route. Realizing that descriptions of this unknown landscape were needed to engage public support for this mission

and that they would be more comprehensible and vividly produced by photographers and illustrators, rather than in the reports of a government scientist, he engaged two new crew members: E.O. Beaman (active 1860–70s), a photographer, and Frederick S. Dellenbaugh (1853–1930), a seventeen-year-old artist who thirty years later chronicled the journey in two popular books. Jack Hillers (1843–1925) was engaged as a boatman but took over the official photographer's duties when Beaman left the group in January 1872 and his replacement, James Fennemore, quit in August 1872 because of poor health. A wet-plate, collodion-based photographic process was to be used to record the images. Because the plates had to be exposed within ten minutes after preparation and developed immediately thereafter, nearly one ton of equipment—darkroom apparatus and chemicals as well as the glass plates and large cameras—had to be moved into position for each shot.[3]

From the beginning there was a symbiotic relationship between the Grand Canyon and its painters and photographers. An inspiration to these artists and a model for their masterpieces, the canyon and its preservation in turn depended upon these artists and photographers who recorded its beauty and so impressed future generations with the need to safeguard it.

The artist-explorers who accompanied Powell, Wheeler, and others on mapping and surveying expeditions in the canyon through the 1870s introduced to Americans the strange topography and landscape of the canyon, helping to incorporate what was still considered alien territory into the popular image of

the United States. Photographers Jack Hillers, William Bell (active 1870s), and Timothy O'Sullivan (c. 1840–1882) illustrated the government reports that first described this area. Beaman, who left the expedition after a dispute with Powell, returned independently and preceded Powell's expedition into the Grand Canyon, becoming the second photographer—following Timothy O'Sullivan on the Wheeler expedition in 1871—to record images of the canyon. Hillers, who left nearly 20,000 negatives with the U.S. Geological Survey and Bureau of American Ethnology, is primarily responsible for popularizing the landscapes and Native cultures of the Southwest.

That the Grand Canyon would become one of the most visited sites in the world—four million tourists from around the world make the journey each year—may have seemed implausible to Major Powell, whose own explorations on horseback and in rigid wooden boats were fraught with peril. To persuade government officials of the importance of protecting this unparalleled site, however, Powell dedicated more of his budget on each expedition to hire great artists and photographers to record its geological features and depict its awe-inspiring vistas. Wheeler, who had graduated from West Point five years earlier—just as the end of the Civil War allowed the Army to direct its resources to other projects—also recognized the value of first-rate imagery for dramatizing this difficult work to its funders. He dedicated one-tenth of his budget for the 1871 U.S. Geological Survey West of the 100th Meridian to equip photographer Timothy O'Sullivan with supplies that included a mobile labo-

LEFT
E.O. Beaman, *Powell Expedition Boats in Marble Canyon*. Courtesy of Grand Canyon National Park.

CENTER
J.K. Hillers, *Looking into Marble Canyon, Shinimo Altar in the Distance*. Courtesy of the National Archives, Washington D.C.

RIGHT
J.K. Hillers, *Lava Falls, Colorado River*. This perilous rapid continues to mesmerize both photographers and river runners. Courtesy of the National Archives, Washington D.C.

< LEFT
William Bell, *Cañon of Kanab Wash, Colorado River, Looking South*, 1872. Courtesy of Amon Carter Museum, Fort Worth.

J.K. Hillers, *Looking north across the cañon from a point on the east side of the Three Castles (Vishnu Quadrangle)*. Courtesy of the National Archives, Washington D.C.

TOP RIGHT
J.K. Hillers, *View in Kanab Creek*. Courtesy of Grand Canyon National Park.

Jack Hillers posed with his photo equipment and mules on the 1872 expedition to survey the Grand Canyon that was led by Major John Wesley Powell.

ratory (made from a military ambulance)—which would prove to be useless in the Grand Canyon passage.

Uniquely qualified for the assignment, O'Sullivan filled with it distinction. At the onset of the Civil War in 1861, he had joined the semiofficial photographic corps led by the master photographer Mathew Brady, to whom he had earlier apprenticed himself. Subsequently he spent three years with another survey team in the Great Basin and served as official photographer on a U.S. Navy expedition to map a canal route in what is now present-day Panama. During the 1871 expedition, Wheeler diverged from his stated mission—which was to focus on the economic and military aspects of the area with "the geologic and natural history branches being treated as incidental to the main purpose"—to journey some 260 miles *up* the Colorado River (against its current), thereby enabling O'Sullivan to make the first photographs of the Grand Canyon. O'Sullivan recorded what Wheeler characterized in his report as "a full and characteristic representation of that very grand and peculiar scenery among the cañons of the Colorado" despite the astounding physical burden of the task and without abandoning his share of the rowing, pushing, portaging, and packing.[4]

William Bell, who replaced O'Sullivan on the 1872 phase of the Wheeler expeditions, continued his fine work but left this report of the difficulty of the assignment:

"I arise at 4 a.m.; feed the mule; shiver down my breakfast; mercury at 30°. . . . If negatives are to be taken on the march, the photographic mule is packed with dark tent, chemical boxes and camera, and out we start ahead of our exploring party on the lookout for views.

Having found a spot from whence three to four views can be had, we make a station, unpack the mule, erect the tent, camera, etc. . . .Troubles are constant, with . . . gusts of wind covering the collodian covered plate with dust and sand until it looks as though it had been sifted . . . from a dredging box"[5]

Hillers, who effused in his diary that he had "photographed all the best scenery"[6] after his first canyon outing on foot, spent August and September of 1872 viewing and shooting the canyon from the river during Powell's expedition. In January and February of 1873 he again photographed the Grand Canyon, realizing a dozen views from the North Rim.

Powell, whose expeditions had brought him national fame, used Hillers's photographs to illustrate his lecture tours. He also derived important funding for his projects by selling rights to reproduce about 650 of the 1,400 stereographs taken during the survey expeditions for home use in the popular stereopticon viewing system. These talks and stereopticon distribution did more to popularize the image of the canyon than the original reports, which were read mainly by government officials. Because halftone printing was not yet available, drawings based on the photographs, not the actual images shot by Beaman, Hillers, and

Fennemore, illustrated Powell's official report to the Smithsonian. The first extensive publication of these photographs was in Dellenbaugh's books, *The Romance of the Colorado River* (1902) and *A Canyon Voyage* (1908), but their reproduction was much inferior to the original photographs.

Long interested in anthropology and America's Native peoples, Powell was appointed Indian Commissioner for the tribes in southern Utah in 1872. By 1873 he had been empowered by the Bureau of Indian Affairs to report on the conditions of Indians throughout canyon country. During the autumn of 1872 and again in the summer of 1873, when Hillers was not engaged in shooting the Grand Canyon for the Powell expedition, he focused on the Kaibab Paiute Indians, who lived part of the year near Kanab, Utah. In early 1876 he returned to photograph the Hopi villages. Both sets of photographs were included in the Centennial Exhibition, which opened in Philadelphia on May 10, 1876, and attracted ten million visitors during its six-month run.

In 1885 Hillers and Powell made their last journeys to the Southwest, marveling at the convenience of the railroad to Flagstaff (which had been completed in 1882) as they traveled to the South Rim for their last view of the Grand Canyon they had so intrepidly explored.

The Kolb Brothers, Emery and Ellsworth, built a photo studio at the head of Bright Angel Trail in 1904 and supported themselves by taking souvenir pictures of tourists. The mule caravans would pause at a vantage point beneath their studio for a shot, then the photographer would run four miles down a trail to process the film at a freshwater source (water was not available at the rim until 1930) and four miles back up to sell the prints when the mule train returned to the rim. The Kolb brothers were not just tourist photographers, but adventurers and artists whose pioneering accomplishments included being only the eighth group to make a successful passage down the Colorado River and the first to make a motion picture of the river trip through the Grand Canyon. Relying on Dellenbaugh's report of the Powell expedition to guide them, the brothers shot on the newly invented Pathé Bray motion picture camera. In his chronicle of their journey, *Through the Grand Canyon from Wyoming to Mexico*, Ellsworth stated the goal of their expedition succinctly:

"The success of our mission depended on our success as photographers. We could not hope to add anything of importance to the scientific and topographic knowledge of the canyons already existing; and merely to come out alive at the other end did not make a strong appeal to our vanity. We were there as scenic photographers in love with their work, and determined to reproduce the marvels of Colorado's canyons, as far as we could do it."

Influenced by the Fred Harvey Corp, which had a longstanding feud with the Kolb brothers, the Park Service agent initially prohibited the showing of the film at Grand Canyon, but for sixty years from 1915,

it was projected twice a day at their studio on the South Rim—introduced and narrated by Emery (in person at first and later on tape). Through this film, generations of tourists experienced vicariously the thrill of riding the wild waters of the Colorado River, realizing the expressed hope of the Kolb brothers: "that we could bring out a record of the Colorado as it is, a live thing, armed as it were with teeth, ready to crush and devour."[7]

By 1912 Ellsworth Kolb recalled the beautiful effects and arduous process of a photographic technique that had already been surpassed by more modern technology:

"The old-fashioned wet plates that had to be coated and developed on the spot [made] wonderful photographs, which for beauty, softness, and detail are not excelled, and are scarcely equalled by more modern plates and photographic results. The only great advantage of the dry plates was the fact that they could catch the action of the water with an instantaneous exposure, where the wet plates had to have a long exposure and lost that action."[8]

The pioneering photographers' works, which deserve to be considered as art, as well as feats of technology and as important documents of the American West, were widely disseminated in government publications, though often misrepresented by poor reproduction. They contain essential information on the Southwest during the early years of its annexation to the United States.

Painterly Visions and Views

*P*AINTERS WORKED under less arduous conditions than photographers because they were not so heavily burdened with equipment and could complete their compositions in the studio. In 1873 Powell hired the great landscape painter Thomas Moran (1837–1926), whose views of Yosemite were credited with helping win congressional protection of that landscape. Powell hoped that Moran's paintings might likewise benefit the Grand Canyon. English born, Moran emigrated to the United States at a young age with his family. His aesthetic sensibility reflects the Luminism developed by Joseph Turner (1775–1851) in London and the metaphysical landscape tradition of the Hudson River School.

Recording his first impressions of the Grand Canyon in a letter to his wife, Moran acknowledged the role of the expedition's photographer, Jack Hillers, in the compositions he would later develop:

> "On reaching the brink the whole gorge lay for miles beneath us and it was by far the most awfully grand and impressive scene that I have ever yet seen....The color of the Grand Cañon itself is red, a light Indian Red, and the material sandstone and red marble and is in terraces all the way down. All above the cañon is variously colored sandstone mainly a light flesh or cream color and worn into very fine forms. I made an outline and did a little color work but had not time nor was it worthwhile to make a detailed study in color. We made several photos which will give me all the details I want if I conclude to paint the view."[9]

Because Moran joined Powell's party late, in the summer of 1873, he missed the river voyage that had already been accomplished and viewed the canyon only from the rim. Moran's great work, *Chasm of the Colorado* (1873), expressed the unique beauty of the place and formed the image of the canyon that remains part of the human imagination. In 1874 Congress appropriated $10,000 for its purchase, and it hung in the Senate lobby at the U.S. Capitol, along with Moran's *Grand Canyon of the Yellowstone*, and kept this extraordinary American landscape before the eyes of Congress until legislation protecting it was passed.[10]

In 1880 Moran and another artist, William Henry Holmes, joined an expedition to explore the Grand Canyon region organized by Clarence Dutton, an expedition that culminated in perhaps the greatest government publication of all time, *Tertiary History of the Grand Cañon District, with Atlas* (1882). Holmes (1846–1933) was a fine draftsman who in his distinguished career was later head curator at the Field Museum and professor of geology at the University of Chicago, replaced Powell as chief of the Bureau of American Ethnology, and in 1910 became the first director of the National Collection of Fine Arts (now the National Gallery of Art).[11]

Dutton's report featured Holmes's panoramic line drawings and precise renderings of the geological formations of the canyon, as well as Moran's more impressionistic landscapes. Moran had memorized the canyon landscape that he loved, a knowledge that impressed Ellsworth Kolb: "Thomas Moran could pick up almost any picture that we made, and tell us at once just what section it came from and its identifying characteristics." But that knowledge was merely the armature on which he built his canvases, which featured dramatic effects of light and space. Holmes was better known for the precision and geological accuracy of his compositions.

The 1880 journey by Holmes and Moran was the last great artistic adventure of the expeditionary phase of the canyon's history; the next generation of artists traveled by railroad in the service of developing tourism. Photographic technology, restricted to black-and-white images, could not express the dramatic colors that have always been a unique feature of the Southwest: its powerful coloration demanded a painter's palette. Paintings by Moran and many other artists were commissioned by the Santa Fe Railroad and used in its advertising and annual calendar to stimulate tourism to the Southwest, an unusually successful case of patronage beneficial to both business and art.

After he was named general advertising manager of the Santa Fe Railroad in 1900, William Haskell

When Teddy Roosevelt visited the Grand Canyon for the first time in 1903, he rode on horseback to dinner at Grandview and, led by legendary guide John Hance, here descends Bright Angel Trail on a mule. Courtesy of Grand Canyon National Park.

Emery and Ellsworth Kolb used the craft of photography to finance life long love affairs with the Grand Canyon. These intrepid explorers hiked throughout the canyon to record its scenery (far left) and worked under arduous field conditions, developing film in a darkroom tent (top left) to make the first motion pictures of the Colorado River journey in 1911–12. Courtesy of Grand Canyon National Park.

The handsome Grand Canyon Lodge, built of Kaibab limestone, seemed to grow out of the North Rim on which it perched. Its opening and the installation of a water-pumping station at Roaring Springs in 1928 made summer tourism to the North Rim comfortable. This hand-tinted Kolb Brothers photograph was made before Grand Canyon Lodge was gutted by fire during the winter of 1932 when the structure was inaccessible because the roads are closed by snow. Courtesy of Grand Canyon National Park. Photograph by D.T. DeDomenico.

Thomas Moran, *Chasm of the Colorado*, 1873. 85 x 145 in.
National Museum of American Art, Smithsonian Institution. Lent by
the U.S. Department of the Interior, Office of the Secretary.

Moran sketching canyon from a rocky perch on the rim.

Simpson (1858–1933) organized month-long painting trips to various scenic areas of the Southwest,
providing rail transportation and lodging at hotels
owned by the Fred Harvey Company, a Santa Fe
subsidiary. In exchange, artists gave the Santa Fe
Railroad at least one painting and its reproduction
rights. In the first ten years of the program the Santa
Fe Railroad acquired more than 250 original paintings; by 1940 it owned 500 paintings.[12]

Moran took his first trip to the canyon under the
aegis of the Santa Fe Railroad in 1892, returning again
in 1901 (when his companions included painter
George Inness, Jr., 1825–94) and almost annually
from 1904 to 1910. The occasion of his last visit to the
Grand Canyon was to participate in what would be a
historic trip in the pictorial life of the canyon. Moran
and four other painters—Elliot Daingerfield (1859–
1932), DéWitt Parshall (1864–1956), Edward
Potthast (1857–1927), and Frederick Ballard Williams (1871–1956)—were accompanied by Nina
Spaulding Stevens, assistant director at the Toledo Art
Museum, whose notes on the trip were later privately
published:

> "The artists were led to the rim with their eyes closed
> that the vision might burst upon them for the first time
> in its entirety....Never before had so large a group of
> serious artists made such a pilgrimage to the Far West
> with the avowed intention of studying a given point of
> their own country, and thus will this visit to the Canyon
> become historical."[13]

Little is known of DeWitt Parshall, but Daingerfield, Potthast, and Williams each visited the Grand Canyon for the first time on this junket. Elliot Daingerfield returned often to the Grand Canyon, and its landscapes became staples of his art. He studied the effects of light and clouds in canvases that show the tradition of the Impressionists and Luminists. Edward Potthast is better known for light-filled paintings of families at the seashore, compositions reminiscent of the Spanish impressionist, Joaquin Sorolla. Frederick Ballard Williams was born in Brooklyn and lived most of his adult life in New Jersey. He returned once again to tour the West.

At El Tovar, the elegant Fred Harvey hotel at the Grand Canyon, works by artists who had enjoyed Santa Fe's patronage were offered for sale in the Art Rooms. A brochure on the hotel, published by Harvey in 1909, boasted: "On the wall hang paintings of Southwest scenery from the brushes of noted American artists, perhaps including one of Thomas Moran's masterpieces, also canvases by Sauerwein, Couse, Sharp, Leigh, Jorgenson, Burgdorff, Wachtel, and Rollins." These artists, although their names are not well known today, gave the Grand Canyon and Southwest culture its first identity for Americans. Their imagery lured travelers into the ticket offices of the Santa Fe Railroad and suggested the delights of travel to patrons at the Harvey-run station restaurants that followed the rail lines from Chicago to the West. The artists shared a pioneer spirit, some settling in art colonies in still-remote outposts, others longing for the dramatic landscape and exotic culture but settling in less isolated centers that offered better prospects for sales.

Frank Paul Sauerwein (1871–1910) sought the desert climate as a remedy for tuberculosis and remained there for the last twenty years of his life to paint the arid landscape he grew to love. His favorite subjects included the Native American culture of the Hopi, but he recognized the financial opportunity of the lucrative tourist trade at the Grand Canyon, where "practically every tourist that crosses the continent stops for a day or more," and was amply rewarded by sales of his work, which was represented by the galleries at El Tovar for several years.[14]

William Robinson Leigh (1866–1955) enjoyed his sobriquet, Sagebrush Rembrandt, and painted dramatic high-toned compositions of the Grand Canyon on frequent visits beginning in 1906. Five of his paintings of the Grand Canyon, which he called one of "the most distinctive characteristic, dramatic, poetic, unique motifs in the world," hung for years at the Harvey hotels on the South Rim.[15]

While still in his teens, Frederick Dellenbaugh had participated in the 1871 Powell expedition and chronicled the journey years later in two very popular books. In the 1880s he painted the villages on Hopi territory, which he was asked to adapt fifty years later as murals for display, along with Hopi artifacts, at the Museum of the American Indian in New York.

Louis Akin (1869–1913) happily left New York City, where he had supported himself as an illustrator, to accept an invitation from the Santa Fe Railroad to paint the Native peoples of the Southwest. He settled on the second floor of an Indian family home in Oraibi, the largest settlement on Hopi tribal lands, in September 1903 and stayed for a year. He described in detail his new surroundings, revealing the fascination they held for him, grown accustomed to Victorian parlors in New York:

"In three corners were tiny, quaint fireplaces, one a sunken oven, and in the other corner the mealing stones, set in a shallow trough in the adobe floor with a wee, unglazed window beside them. A broad, low banquette on one side offered a cozy couching place with another half partition at one end, giving it semiprivacy. Then there were sundry cubby holes in the walls and a couple of storage bins which furnished seating space. The walls were smoothly plastered with adobe by hand, in a way that leaves no square corners or hard, straight lines, and all but the floor was neatly whitewashed with pure, white clay."[16]

Akin returned to New York but could no longer reconcile himself to urban life. By 1906 he had returned to the Southwest, settling in Flagstaff and traveling often to the South Rim of the Grand Canyon and the Hopi lands. A painting by Akin was commissioned to announce the opening of El Tovar; he devised a composition that featured Native Americans strolling along the rim and a precipitous view into a pastel-hued canyon. The image was widely reproduced on Santa Fe Railroad's advertising and hung in its ticket offices throughout the United States. Akin returned again and again to scenes of the canyon for his compositions: his biographer, Arizona Governor Bruce Babbitt, estimates that one-quarter of Akin's

Thomas Moran, whose views of Yosemite had helped win it congressional protection, was engaged by Major Powell in 1873 with the expectation that his paintings might likewise benefit the Grand Canyon. This view of the east end of the canyon shows a cold-air inversion that has trapped clouds beneath the rim. Courtesy of Grand Canyon National Park. Photograph by D.T. DeDomenico.

William Henry Holmes, "Panorama from Point Sublime," three panels, from *Tertiary History of the Grand Cañon District, with Atlas*. Photograph by Dana Levy.

finished works depicted the canyon. A huge canyon view by Akin has hung for several decades at Verkampf's gift shop across from El Tovar.

Swedish-born Gunnar Widforss (1879–1934) was one of the first painters to be sponsored by the National Park Service (which was established in 1916). Its director, Stephen T. Mather, encouraged Widforss to specialize in painting the national parks—a challenge he met with such skill that his work was the subject of a 1924 retrospective at the National Gallery of Art (whose director, William Holmes, shared a long-standing interest in the subject). Widforss lived at the Grand Canyon during the 1920s and 1930s, where he painted—often working in watercolor—clear and precise views from both the South Rim and the canyon floor, depicting accurately its geology and formations.[17]

A Source for Modern Photography

*W*HILE THE LUMINIST PAINTERS and their heirs recorded the canyon, often under the patronage of the Santa Fe Railroad, a generation of photographers attempted "to draw or paint by light." Pictorialism was a photographic movement that repudiated the objective nature of the medium, stressing instead the ability of the camera to convey the mood and emotion of both artist and subject. Rejecting the standardization of printing that evolved with developing technology, these photographers returned to older processes, manipulating their images in the darkroom. Landscape, the more pastoral the better, was a subject well suited to pictorialist technique, and several masters of this style selected the Grand Canyon as one of their subjects.[18]

Alvin Langdon Coburn (1882–1966), a founding member of the American Photo-Secession with Alfred Steiglitz and longtime friend of Edward Steichen, visited the Grand Canyon in autumn 1911 and returned in January 1912 with painter Arthur Wesley Dow, his former teacher. The subject and not the pleasures of Grand Canyon travel attracted these artists, as this account from Coburn's journal attests: "When I crawled into my sleeping-bag I had to encircle myself with a horse-hair rope to keep out the rattle-snakes. Horse-hair tickled them, so they left you alone."[19] Coburn believed that the Grand Canyon pictures were among the best photographs he ever made.

Identified with the soft-focus pictorial style, Karl Struss (1886–1981) contributed a lens to its technical development. He had studied with Clarence White at Columbia University and ran White's studio from 1914 to 1917, before leaving New York for the West Coast. En route, like many travelers, Struss stopped at the Grand Canyon and made several photographs, including one that captured a prize in a major exhibition of pictorial photography in 1921. Settling in Hollywood, he became Cecil B. DeMille's preferred cinematographer and won the first Academy Award for cinematography for the 1927 film *Sunrise*.[20]

Ansel Adams (1902–84) was associated for sixty years with Sierra Club and became the best-known champion for preservation of certain important natural sites in the West—notably Yosemite and Big Sur. In 1941–42 Adams photographed the Grand Canyon and other national parks for a mural project directed by the U.S. Department of the Interior, a project that was never realized because of the onset of World War II. Adams's photographs, capturing both panoramic vistas and close-up details of the parks, were intended to supplement the painted murals that had been commissioned.

Among modern photographers, Eliot Porter (1901–1990) is identified with environmental protests over construction of the Glen Canyon Dam, which forever changed the ecology of the Colorado River. Because of Porter's landmark book, *The Place No One Knew: Glen Canyon on the Colorado*, his "name will be inseparable from the spirit of Glen Canyon, just as John Wesley Powell's is from the discovery of the canyon," David Brower, then head of the Sierra Club, wrote in the introduction to that volume.[21] Although his photographs of the fragile ecology of this rare place failed to halt construction of the dam, Porter's work endeared him forever to

environmentalists, who took up the cause to prevent construction of other proposed dams further along the Colorado River. To commemorate the centenary of Powell's first expedition, Porter published a portfolio of his images of the canyon and Colorado River, accompanied by excerpts from Powell's journal.

Mark Klett (born 1952) traveled with other photographers throughout the Southwest in the late 1970s, searching for the vantage points from which early expedition photographers had recorded their images. Although their work, published as *Second View: The Rephotographic Survey Project* (University of New Mexico Press, 1984), revealed the effects of a century of human impact on the landscape, the an-

cient scenery of the Grand Canyon seems immutable. Klett framed his five-panel panorama from Toroweap with views initially recorded by Jack Hillers, but the original composition is marked with a telltale insignia of the photographer—Klett's hat in the foreground. In the catalogue of the National Gallery of Art's survey of the first 150 years of photography, Colin Westerbeck suggested that: "Klett has elided the pictorial history of the West with later commercial developments by manipulating dye-transfer color prints to achieve the tinted look of nineteenth- and early twentieth-century postcards." Photography for exploration and for tourism are thus merged in Klett's work.[22]

The Grand Canyon continues to inspire each generation of photographers, including the nine whose works are featured in this book.

David Muench studied photography at the Rochester Institute of Technology in New York and at the Art Center School of Design in California where his love for nature and the landscape became his most satisfying form of photographic expression. Muench developed his photographic style while making photographs for his stock collection and for such magazines as *National Geographic, Audubon, Buzzworm, Sierra, Trilogy,* and *Wilderness.* More recently he has concentrated on self-assigned subjects for exhibition or book publication. *Nature's America, Anasazi: Ancient People of the Rock, Uncommon Places,* and monographs on several western states are recent publications. A permanent installation of his photographs illustrates the Lewis and

Clark expeditions of 1804-1806, and serves as a gateway to the west in Saint Louis. His photographs are also the subject of an exhibition, "Ancient America," organized by the Santa Barbara Museum of Art, which will travel to other cities beginning in 1993.

Arriving in Flagstaff in 1965 to attend Northern Arizona University, where he took his degree in anthropology, John Running promptly "fell in love with the people and the area." His work is centered mainly on people, documenting them in the work place. He is known for sensitive portraiture of Native Americans, but his images of corporate chiefs are equally adept. When deadlines or interactions with human subjects become taxing, he finds nature photography therapeutic. He joins scientific expeditions as photographer or volunteers as a boatman to ensure a river passage through the Grand Canyon at least once each year.

Tom Bean studied wildlife biology at college in his native Iowa and began his professional life as a seasonal park ranger in the Black Hills of South Dakota. Photographing wildlife to illustrate his ranger talks, he continued to take pictures during six seasons at Glacier Bay and Denali national parks in Alaska. The work of David Cavagnero in such books as *Living Earth* and *Living Water* was an early inspiration because it focused on intimate details, not obvious big scenery, and revealed a different perspective on landscape. Finding the Alaskan wilderness was too remote to run a photography business, Bean relocated to Flagstaff in 1982. He now roams far afield on

assignments for *Audubon, Life, National Geographic, Traveler, Travel & Leisure,* and many natural history journals. He has published a book on Lava Beds National Monument and *Along the Rim,* an itinerary for tourists to the South Rim of the Grand Canyon, and contributed to several National Geographic books.

Dana Levy studied at the Art Center School of Design in the 1960s and began his career in graphic design in Japan. *Bamboo* and *Water: A View from Japan,* both photographic studies of the natural world, were followed by *Kanban: Shop Signs of Japan* and *Furo: The Japanese Bath,* which focused on aspects of Japanese culture. In addition to editing photos and designing *The Grand Canyon,* he traveled to the site with a special panorama-format camera to make large horizontal compositions. He looks forward to making a river voyage through the Grand Canyon with his new son.

During eight summers when he worked as a boatman for Grand Canyon Dories, John Blaustein

In his journal, Hillers described how he made this *"picture showing the whole Cañon. For this purpose we climbed halfway down—showing the river for nearly three miles and the walls 2000 feet below and 3000 feet above."* This view from Toroweap has remained compelling to modern photographers, including Mark Klett, who used a similar composition for the first panel of *Around Toroweap Point, just before and after sunset, beginning and ending with views by J.K. Hillers over 100 years ago, Grand Canyon,* 1986. Courtesy of the artist and the Amon Carter Museum, Fort Worth.

In the 1940s, Ansel Adams worked on a photo mural project for the Department of the Interior, which was interrupted by World War II and never realized. These photographs, now in the collection of the National Archives include this view up Bright Angel Canyon from the South Rim (top). Adams traveled frequently in Arizona, returning to the canyon in 1952 when the view (bottom left) was shot. Courtesy of National Archives, Washington D.C.

TOP LEFT
Karl Struss, *The Canyon, Late afternoon,* 1919. Courtesy of the Amon Carter Museum, Fort Worth

BOTTOM RIGHT
A 1911 view of canyon formations by Alvin Langdon Coburn, who worked during this period in the Pictorialist style. Courtesy of International Museum of Photography at George Eastman House, Rochester.

focused on rapids and riverine views. The combination of landscape and white water drew him back summer after summer: "As the roughest stretch of navigable water in America, it is the ultimate roller-coaster ride, and it is fortuitously located at the base of the Grand Canyon, which is the ultimate scenery." He had the good fortune to draw photographer Ernst Haas as a passenger on an early trip and was inspired by their two-week discussion to pursue a professional career. Many of Blaustein's Grand Canyon photographs were published, with an essay by Edward Abbey, in *The Hidden Canyon: A River Journey* (Viking Penguin, 1977). A commercial photographer based in Berkeley, California, he specializes in advertising and annual reports.

Greg Probst developed his color photography on a 4x5 camera during the three years he lived on the South Rim as a staff photographer and lab technician for the National Park Service at the Grand Canyon. To establish a private practice in nature and stock photography, he returned to his native Seattle where he is

Left

Eliot Porter. *Seven Mile Canyon, Glen Canyon*, shot September 2, 1962. Courtesy of Amon Carter Museum, Fort Worth.

Right

Eliot Porter, *View up the Colorado from Toroweap Point*, shot August 13, 1969. Courtesy of Amon Carter Museum, Fort Worth.

NOTES

1. Michael Collier, *An Introduction to Grand Canyon Geology.* Grand Canyon Natural History Association, 1980.
2. J. Donald Hughes, *In the House of Stone and Light.* Grand Canyon Natural History Association, 1978.
3. Don D. Fowler, *The Western Photographs of John K. Hillers.* Smithsonian Institution Press, 1989.
4. *Wheeler's Photographic Survey of the American West, 1871-1873.* Dover Publications, 1983.
5. James K. Ballinger and Andrea D. Rubinstein, *Visitors to Arizona 1846 to 1980.* Phoenix Art Museum, 1980, n.p.
6. Fowler 1989, p. 23.
7. Ellsworth L. Kolb, *Through the Grand Canyon from Wyoming to Mexico.* Macmillan, 1914; reprinted by the University of Arizona Press, 1989.
8. William C. Suran, *The Kolb Brothers of the Grand Canyon.* Grand Canyon Natural History Association, 1991.
9. *Home-Thoughts from Afar: Letters of Thomas Moran to Mary Nimmo Moran.* East Hampton Free Library, 1967.
10. *Splendors of the American West: Thomas Moran's Art of the Grand Canyon and Yellowstone.* Birmingham Museum of Art in association with the University of Washington Press, 1990. The author would like to thank Charles Robertson, Deputy Director of the National Museum of American Art, for making it possible to include a reproduction of *Chasm of the Colorado* in this volume.
11. *Capturing the Canyon.* The Mesa Southwest Museum, 1987, n.p.
12. Sandra D'Emilio and Suzan Campbell, *Visions and Visionaries: The Art and Artists of the Santa Fe Railway.* Peregrine Smith Books, 1991.
13. Microfilm roll #1124, Archives of American Art, Smithsonian Institution, as quoted in Ballinger and Rubinstein 1980.
14. Sauerwein, as quoted in Ballinger and Rubinstein 1980.
15. D'Emilio and Campbell 1991, p. 32.
16. Bruce E. Babbitt, *Color and Light: The Southwest Canvases of Louis Akin.* Northland Press, 1973.
17. *Capturing the Canyon*, 1987.
18. Sarah Greenough, "The Curious Contagion of the Camera," in *On the Art of Fixing a Shadow.* National Gallery of Art and the Art Institute of Chicago, 1989.
19. Ballinger and Rubinstein 1980.
20. The author would like to thank Barbara McCandless, Assistant Curator of Photography at the Amon Carter Museum, for information on Struss and for assistance in procuring photographs.
21. Eliot Porter, *The Place No One Knew: Glen Canyon on the Colorado.* Sierra Club, 1963; reprinted by Peregrine Smith Books, 1983.
22. Colin Westerbeck, "Beyond the Photographic Frame," in *On the Art of Fixing a Shadow*, 1989.
23. *New York Sun*, May 7, 1903.

represented by Allstock. Probst, the youngest of the featured photographers, travels widely through the western states and Canada.

Although he makes his publishing debut in this book, Paul Vucetich's photographs have been a resource for rangers and naturalists at the Grand Canyon where he worked for four summers. From his base on the North Rim, Vucetich hikes into the canyon, focusing on the flora and fauna, as well as the larger views that are so compelling. He is a self-taught photographer who began to practice his craft at age eleven when a family friend gave him darkroom equipment. Wilderness areas, including the national forests and mountain ranges in Montana, are subjects of interest to him.

D.T. DeDomenico inaugurates a new career with this publication. He studied European history and practiced law and business for a decade in the Bay Area before embarking on a new course by enrolling in the photography program at California College of Arts and Crafts. He lost his home in the 1991 Oakland fire,

but is undeterred from his goals: to be published by *Aperture* and *National Geographic*, like William Albert Allard, whose color style and work with people he admires.

Michael Collier divides his time between photography and medicine, working as a family practice physician in Flagstaff. He initially trained as a geologist, taking his undergraduate degree at Northern Arizona University and his master's at Stanford. He applied his expertise in geology to the Grand Canyon in a very readable and informative small book, *An Introduction to Grand Canyon Geology* (Grand Canyon Natural History Association, 1980). From 1975 he worked for several summers as a boatman on river trips through the Grand Canyon, but as a photographer he prefers an aerial perspective from which he can view the geologic formations that have shaped this region. Collier's work in *Arizona: A View from Above* (Westcliffe, 1990) reveals many facets and formations of the Grand Canyon.

Like most visitors, these photographers, enthralled

by the Grand Canyon's unique beauty, have taken to heart Teddy Roosevelt's stirring plea, which he enunciated in 1903, standing at the rim of the canyon he would later help to preserve:

"In the Grand Canyon, Arizona has a natural wonder which, so far as I know, is in kind absolutely unparalleled throughout the rest of the world. I want to ask you to do one thing in connection with it, in your own interest and in the interest of the country—to keep this great wonder of nature as it is now....The ages have been at work on it and man can only mar it. What you can do is to keep it for your children, your children's children, and for all who come after you, as the one great sight which every American who can travel at all should see."[23]

TOURISM AT THE GRAND CANYON

by Rena Zurofsky

Passengers on the first train disembark at the South Rim, 1901.

Restored trains were introduced, after a twenty-year hiatus, in 1990, so passengers again disembark near El Tovar. Photograph by D.T. DeDomenico.

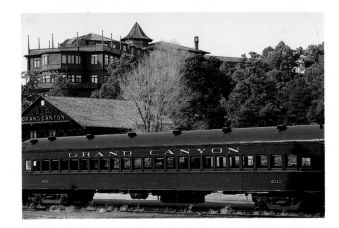

I N 1857 LIEUTENANT JOSEPH C. IVES, leader of a government survey to determine the navigability of the Colorado River, was sanguine neither about those prospects nor about the potential for tourism to the Grand Canyon: "Ours has been the first, and will doubtless be the last, party of whites to visit this profitless locality. It seems intended by nature that the Colorado River, along the greater portion of its lonely and majestic way, shall be forever unvisited and undisturbed." [1]

These days about four million tourists visit the Grand Canyon each year, proving the earnest lieutenant to have suffered from poverty of imagination. Starting with government surveyors including Ives and Major John Wesley Powell (who was a good deal more appreciative), to prospectors, developers, adventurers to just ordinary folks, Americans and foreigners have gone to great lengths and sometimes considerable expense to visit the lieutenant's "profitless locality."

A system of transportation and lodging developed steadily, despite remote and difficult terrain. Tourism grew at the canyon because of lively entrepreneurial spirit and the federal government's cooperation. Word of mouth—and pen—was vital, too. From a nineteenth-century traveler's "Horror! Tragedy! Silence! Death! Chaos! There is the awful canyon in five words!" [2] to more favorable reviews, visitors have said things about the place that just make others want to see it for themselves.

Getting There

T HE FIRST STEP toward general accessibility was the completion in 1882 of the local portion of the Santa Fe Railroad's cross-continental train line. Passengers who'd slept in clean new Pullman cars disembarked at Flagstaff and continued their journey by stagecoach, a trip that averaged eleven hours, included three relay changes and at least one meal.

In 1891 essayist Charles Dudley Warner described the trip:

"Flagstaff is the best present point of departure...The distance [to the South Rim] is seventy-six miles through a practically uninhabited country, much of it a desert, and with water very infrequent...a good deal of it is intolerably dusty or exceedingly stony...a tiresome journey of two days...This will cost the traveler, according to the size of the party made up, from forty to fifty dollars." [3]

In 1899 Chicago poet Harriet Monroe reinforced the dreariness of the journey:

"The immense and endless desolation seemed to efface us from the earth. What right had we there, on those lofty lands which never since the beginning of time had offered sustenance to man?...At last we reach the third relay station, and take on six horses instead of four, for the final pull uphill...We reflect that as we are traveling now, even in this primitive slavery to beasts of burden, so for many centuries our fathers had traversed the earth, knowing no swifter way. All day for seventy-five miles—yet through ages and ages the lords of the earth had been so deaf to its voices that not one secret of

nature's power had escaped to help them conquer her. We had left the nineteenth century behind; we were exploring the wilderness with the pioneers...." [4]

Eliminating the grueling stagecoach journey proved to be the single most important event in the development of the tourist industry at the canyon. September 17, 1901, the first scheduled passenger train journeyed to the Grand Canyon from Williams, Arizona. The sixty-four–mile train ride to Grand Canyon Village took three hours and cost $3.95. The following year John Muir commended the Santa Fe for its limited environmental impact: "When I first heard of the Santa Fe trains running to the edge of the Grand Cañon of the Arizona, I was troubled with thoughts of the disenchantment likely to follow. But last winter, when I saw those trains crawling along through the pines of the Coconino forest and close up to the brink of the chasm at Bright Angel, I was glad to discover that in the presence of such stupendous scenery they are nothing. The locomotives and trains are mere beetles and caterpillars, and the noise they make is as little disturbing as the hooting of an owl in the lonely woods." [5]

In 1902 the first automobile was driven to the canyon's South Rim by a Los Angeles native, Oliver Lippincott. The car had been built by the Toledo Automobile Company and sent to Flagstaff for the trip. It was a ten-horsepower steam machine, with a coil boiler and gasoline fuel. Lippincott and his companions, two writers and a guide, anticipated a seven-hour drive when they started off on the afternoon of January 4, but they did not arrive until two days later, "and not a particle of food did we have to eat, nor a drop of water to drink, until we got there." [6]

It was 1907 before an automobile attempted to reach the North Rim, a feat that required three days of driving from Utah. Trains remained the preferred mode of travel until the 1930s, when the automobile became the more common choice. Ever since the Grand Canyon Railway suspended its service in 1968, when only three people boarded its last run, the Grand Canyon parking lots have expanded to accommodate more than one million vehicles per year (with their unavoidable pollution).

The train from Williams was reintroduced in 1990, restored with a measure of historic accuracy. Although it carries only 500 passengers a day, it transported 75,000 passengers in its first year. The idea now is to encourage a more ecologically aware tourist trade, so that visitors will choose to leave their cars at home (or at least at the train station sixty-four miles away from the canyon.)

Staying There

T HE FIRST INDIVIDUAL who catered to travelers, John D. Lee, set up a ferry operation at the junction of the Paria and Colorado rivers in 1872. According to Mark Twain, in *Roughing It*, Lee was an adopted son of Brigham Young's who had settled in this remote area expecting that tempers would cool down following the particularly cruel Mountain Mead-

ows Massacre, which Lee was said to have led. The massacre occurred in 1857, when a wagon train from Arkansas and Missouri was attacked in Mountain Meadows, Utah, by Mormons and Indians. Lee claimed he had nothing to do with the incident. He remained safe long enough to have been surprised, no doubt, by his trial and execution in 1877. At the time of his trial, Lee had been host to members of the Powell expedition who'd been waiting a month for the arrival of the Major. James Fennemore, the expedition's photographer, took a last photo of Lee seated atop his coffin, awaiting his end. One of Lee's nineteen wives—Emma—kept the ferry going after his death. An apparently less colorful character, Harrison Pearce, established a ferry at the western end of the Canyon in 1876.

In 1884 the first hotel, called the Farlee, opened for business near Diamond Creek. It had two bedrooms. The Farlee closed its simple operation in 1889 but another, larger tourist facility was opened at Dripping Springs by Louis D. Boucher. At about this time prospectors opened up the Bright Angel Trail following an old Havasupai Indian Route.

The next year, William Wallace Bass, a poet seeking refuge from his job on the New York City elevated

train lines, opened a camp for tourists. It consisted of one small central building containing a dining room, sitting room, kitchen, and several bedrooms. Tent houses and tent stables were used for further accommodations. Bass also reworked the old Havasupai Trail and built a canvas boat to carry people across the river. He constructed another tent camp along the Shinumo Creek drainage. A Bass Camp pamphlet printed around 1906 advertised : "Wonderful Scenic Features/Well Engineered Trail/Ferry Cable across the Colorado River/Trail on the North Side to Point Sublime and Powell Plateau/Camp Garden on the Shinumo/The Natural Place to outfit for Trip to Havasu Canyon/The Havasupai Indians and Waterfalls." Rates were $2.50 a day. The hotel was twenty miles west from Bass Station (Ash Fork) of the Grand Canyon Railway. Bass constructed the road himself so that he could carry people by stage.

In 1886 a miner named John Hance opened his ranch near Grandview to tourists. Nine years later he sold his ranch and began a long career as a Grand Canyon guide. Hance was a born storyteller, a wily inventor of tall tales about the canyon. A guest at his ranch wrote "God made the canyon, John Hance the trail; without the other, neither would be complete."

The pace of development increased during the 1890s. President Benjamin Harrison accomplished in 1893 what he, as Senator, had failed to do in previous years, and that was to declare the Grand Canyon a National Forest Preserve. At the same time, the Santa Fe railroad's publicity campaign began to stimulate general tourism.

Other hotels sprang up. The Grand Canyon Hotel Company incorporated in 1892 to build necessary eating houses en route to the canyon by stage. The Bright Angel Hotel was opened 1896 by the same man who purchased Hance's Grandview place. That same year, Hance became postmaster at the local station, named Tourist; and John George Verkamp opened a curio store in a tent. In 1903 the Cameron Hotel began to operate in Grand Canyon Village; its owner controlled and turned into a toll road the Bright Angel Trail. But all of this activity was a simple prelude to the main event: just as the railway worked an exponential change on the canyon's accessibility, the El Tovar changed the experience of a sojourn there.

The El Tovar hotel opened in 1905 within steps of the railroad terminus on the rim of the canyon near the Bright Angel Trail. It cost $250,000 to build (stables were another $50,000). El Tovar (named for Don Pedro de Tovar, who, it was said, had learned of the canyon from the Hopis and so informed Coronado) was the centerpiece of the facilities so carefully developed by the Santa Fe Railroad and operated by its chief concessionaire, the Fred Harvey Company, which runs it still. British-born Fred Harvey opened his first restaurant in Kansas in 1876, but ultimately became known as the "Civilizer of the West" by operating restaurants, hotels, newsstands, and dining cars for the Railroad:

"The original Fred Harvey is dead—has been dead, in fact, for several years; but his spirit goes marching on across the southwestern half of...this country. Two thousand miles from salt water, the oysters that are served on his dining cars do not seem to be suffering from car-sickness. And you can get a beefsteak measuring eighteen inches from tip to tip....There is another detail of the Harvey system that makes you wonder. Out on the desert, in a dead-gray expanse of silence and sagebrush, your train halts at a junction point that you never even heard of before. There is not much to be seen...except that, right out there in the middle of nowhere, stands a hotel big enough and handsome enough for Chicago or New York, built in the Spanish style, with wide patios and pergolas, where a hundred persons might perg at one time, and gay striped awnings. It is flanked by flower-beds and refreshingly green strips of lawn, with spouting fountains scattered about."[7]

The El Tovar is a rambling structure built with native boulders and pine logs from Oregon and decorated with the rustic elegance of the arts and crafts movement. The hotel was designed by Mary Elizabeth Jane Colter, who gave her unifying vision to all of the Fred Harvey facilities built at the canyon.

El Tovar opened to accommodate two hundred guests. It had a Rendezvous room, decorated with animal heads and Indian crafts, and Art Rooms, where some paintings and photographs commissioned by the Santa Fe Railroad were offered for sale. The Norway Dining Room, 89 feet long by 38 feet wide, was served by well-trained Harvey Girl waitresses and an Italian chef. The hotel boasted a music room, two roof gardens, a sun parlor, an amusement room, a club room, and a barber shop. Stables accommodated 125 animals in addition to coaches and wagons.

For guests who wanted to spend the night at the bottom of the canyon, there was Rust's Camp and the camp at the bottom of Hermit Trail, ten miles west of Bright Angel, which Irvin Cobb described in 1913 as:

"This was roughing it de-luxe with a most de-luxey vengeance! Here were three tents or rather three canvas houses, with wooden half-walls; and they were spic-and-span inside and out, and had glass windows in them and doors and matched wooden floors. The one that was bedrooom had gay Navajo blankets on the floor, and a stove in it, and a little bureau, and a washstand with white towels and good lathery soap. And there were two beds, not cots or bunks, but regular beds, with wire springs and mattresses and white sheets and pillowslips. They were not veteran sheets and vintage pillowslips either, but clean and spotless ones. The mess tent was provided with a table with a clean cloth to go over it, and there were china dishes and china cups and shiny knives, forks and spoons....outside there was a corral for the mules; a canvas storehouse; a hitching stake for the burros; a Dutch oven, and a little forge where the guides sometimes shoe a mule."[8]

In 1907 a cable car was installed across the Colorado River at Rust's Camp, near the mouth of Bright Angel Creek. A year later President Theodore Roosevelt declared the Grand Canyon a National Monument. In 1912 Arizona became the 48th state and West Rim Drive was completed. Rust's Camp was renamed Roosevelt's camp in honor of Teddy's 1913 visit there.

The National Park Service was established in 1916.

In 1920 the Service declared the Fred Harvey Company to be the principal park concessionaire on the South Rim. They bought Bass out of business, turned Roosevelt's camp into Phantom Ranch (1922), and constructed other tourist accommodations.

Tourist development on the North Rim began in 1917. The North Rim is generally less accessible than the South Rim and due to severe winter is closed from November to April. It wasn't until 1926 that paved roads reached the area. The Utah Parks Company, a subsidiary of the Union Pacific Railroad, opened the Grand Canyon Lodge for business in 1928. Designed by Gilbert Stanley Underwood, architect of the famous Ahwahnee Hotel at Yosemite, the hotel consisted of a main building, one hundred standard and twenty-five deluxe cabins. To supply water to the Lodge, a 12,500-foot pipeline was constructed from a water pumping station and power generating plant built 3,870 feet below the rim near Roaring Springs. In 1932 much of the Grand Canyon Lodge burned to the ground during the inaccessible winter season, and it wasn't until 1937 that a reconstructed Lodge reopened. It is now managed by TW Recreation Services.

During the 1920s and 1930s development continued apace. A suspension bridge was put up to connect the north and south Kaibab Trails in 1921. It was replaced with a rigid span in 1928. Bright Angel Lodge opened on the South Rim in 1935. Also on the South Rim, the National Park Service developed an Auto Camp Lodge, public campgrounds complete with an information bureau, a reference library. They also rented blankets and linens to those who arrived unprepared for an overnight stay.

These days, in peak season the Park Service employs 300 people, and twenty-eight concessionaires employ a total of 1,500 workers. They are all hard-pressed to handle the ever-increasing mobs. By 1956 there were one million annual visitors. Another million was added by the end of the next decade, and another by the end of each subsequent decade. While the 1,181 lodging units, 88 trailer sites, and 462 rim campsites are too many for nature lovers, they are hardly enough to handle each year's 3.9 million tourists on the South Rim, and another 350,000 tourists during the five-month season on the North Rim.

Exploring the Canyon

THE TYPICAL VISITOR TODAY spends about three hours at the canyon. Many tourists simply stand at the top around mile 89 (Bright Angel Trail, the railway terminus, and hotels) and stare at the view. As John Muir noted in 1902:

"...I have observed scenery-hunters of all sorts getting first views of Yosemites, glaciers, White Mountain ranges, etc. Mixed with the enthusiasm which such scenery naturally excites, there is often weak gushing, and many splutter aloud like little waterfalls. Here, for a few moments at least, there is silence, and all are in dead earnest, as if awed and hushed by an earthquake—perhaps until the cook cries 'breakfast!' or the stable-

George Grant, a staff photographer for the National Park Service at Grand Canyon, shot these views of staff singing to busloads of departing visitors (opposite) and waitresses on the porch of Grand Canyon Lodge (left) in July 1930. Courtesy of Grand Canyon National Park. Photograph by D.T. DeDomenico.

The outdoor fireplace, on the terrace overlooking the canyon, still draws visitors to Grand Canyon Lodge on the North Rim. Courtesy of Grand Canyon National Park. Photograph by D.T. DeDomenico.

TOP

Rust's aerial tramway, a cable crossing to Rust's camp on the north side of the river, was built in 1907. Ellsworth Kolb is seated at left. Courtesy of Grand Canyon National Park.

BOTTOM

Two guests are served a meal by proprietor David Rust at his camp on Bright Angel Creek. Courtesy of Grand Canyon National Park.

boy 'horses are ready!' Then the poor unfortunates, slaves of regular habits, turn quickly away, gasping and muttering as if wondering where they had been and what had enchanted them." [9]

To provide access to the trails and ease congestion, the hotels improved upon old Indian and prospector paths and added roads for hikers, stages (and ultimately cars and tour buses) around the rim. The more adventurous could make arrangements through the hotels for trail riding, during the day or overnight. Some rides hugged the rim of the canyon visiting cliff houses or limestone caves to hunt for pottery shards; but by far the most piquant outing was—and for about twenty thousand people annually still is—a trip into the canyon on top of a mule.

Even before the El Tovar opened, John Muir noted:

"...a surprising number go down the Bright Angel trail to the brink of the inner gloomy granite gorge over looking the river. Deep cañons attract like high mountains; the deeper they are, the more surely are we drawn into them. On foot, of course there is no danger whatever, and, with ordinary precautions, but little on animals...By the Bright Angel trail the last fifteen hundred feet of the descent to the river has to be made afoot down the gorge of Indian Garden Creek. Most of the visitors do not like this part, and are content to stop at the end of the horse-trail and look down on the dull-brown flood from the edge of the Indian Garden Plateau. By the new Hance trail [mile 77], excepting a few daringly steep spots, you can ride all the way to the river. This trail, built by brave Hance, begins on the highest part of the rim, eight thousand feet above the sea, a thousand feet higher than the head of Bright Angel trail, and the descent is a little over six thousand feet." [10]

John Hance, himself, frequently acted as guide. He is also sometimes credited with introducing mules to the canyon. El Tovar mass-marketed mule touring, providing divided skirts for the ladies. The energetic Kolb Brothers offered their photographic services as well. In 1909 the Fred Harvey Company published a little pamphlet by John McCutcheon, a humorist and cartoonist that described the mule ride:

"A short way below the rim occurs the first adventure. The caravan is halted while a young man takes a photograph of the crowd. When you return in the evening finished copies will be ready for you, if you wish to purchase them....The photographer is very crafty, for he posts his camera in a position overhead that makes the trail look twice as steep as it really is. And that will please you, for in after years when you tell your friends about the memorable ride, you can show them how steep the trail was, and how daring you must necessarily have been to plunge down those ice-bound ledges. Usually, however, the presence in the photograph of some peaceful old lady detracts much from the heroism and daredevil character of your ride." [11]

Most tourists just rode down and up in a single day, and El Tovar kept evening activities going. The management was not above staging "cowboy" whooping and shouting for tourists who'd expected to see some of that romantic stuff. John Hance might come around to tell some tall tales.

By 1915 Ellsworth and Emery Kolb had also installed a movie theatre where they twice daily showed the film they'd made of their 1911–12 Colorado River run, only the eighth run on record. Their movie was one of the most popular and educational activities at the South Rim. And, of course, everyone engaged in the all-time most popular tourist activity: "Each table is thronged by busy writers. It is the picture-post-card hour, and people are writing cards to everybody they know." [12]

Today there are museums and visitor centers, and an Imax theatre right outside the park featuring a reenactment of Major Powell's harrowing river run. Tourists may take guide-conducted hikes and bus rides. Helicopter trips and other air tours over the canyon, while expensive, draw some 700,000 passengers a year. In 1956 flights were severely limited to a narrow corridor after two airliners crashed, killing all people on board. Flights may eventually be eliminated in the effort to control smog and noise pollution.

Each year, some 800,000 tourists enter the inner canyon by foot but, with fewer than 100,000 overnights registered, most stay fairly close to the rims on the main corridor trails, primarily Bright Angel and the North and South Kaibabs. Hiking is the ideal option for those craving a quieter communion with nature, but extreme temperatures and the general lack of water demand careful planning for both hiking and camping. Even the well-used Bright Angel Trail consists of sharp dirt switchbacks that are tricky to negotiate, particularly once the sun begins to flatten out all of the surrounding surfaces towards the middle of the day. Unfortunately, many enter the canyon unprepared. On any summer day you might see people straggle back up the trail stripped to their underwear, or barefoot because their feet blistered.

More than four hundred search-and-rescues were executed during the 1991 season. By far the two most prevalent conditions were dehydration (62) and heat exhaustion (41). Plain old exhaustion hovers near the third spot (21) right behind a fractured ankle (22). Forty-six of the rescues were considered to have saved a life; and nearly half of all attempts were done by helicopter, though wind currents, tight spaces, and the swift fall of darkness into the canyon make this form of rescue dangerous.

A remarkable example of responsible hiking was executed by the intrepid Colin Fletcher, who in the 1960s walked two hundred miles through the canyon and published in 1967 a highly detailed, practical, and mystical chronicle of his journey that continues to inspire many ambitious hikers to meet the challenges of the canyon. Of course, many others had spent substantial time hiking throughout the canyon; for instance, Fletcher learned a lot about the best trails and where he would find water from Harvey Butchart, the local college math professor who at intervals over many years has hiked 1,500 miles in the canyon and written extensively about it. But Fletcher craved a total immersion in the place from his first sight of it:

"Long before we came close, I saw the space...An impossible, breath-taking gap in the face of the earth. And up from this void shone a soft, luminous light...And there, defeating my senses, was the depth. The depth and the distances...And stamped across everything, a master pattern." [13]

Fletcher was, already, a compulsive walker. It took a year for him to prepare, but ultimately—carrying a sixty-pound pack and picking up cached and dropped supplies along the way—he forged a path in two months from Hualapai Hilltop on the South Rim east to the Nankoweap Creek area on the North Rim, from one end of the National Park to the other:

"And all the time the cliff was almost overwhelming me with its bulk and beauty and threat. Its bulk, because there was nothing else beyond my right shoulder: just the unbearable weight of solid rock. Its beauty, because time and the river had sculptured the whole cliff face into snaggle-toothed projections, each shape sharp and angular, each surface smooth, each pattern a dazzle-contrast of deep rich red and, where a projection blocked the setting sun, almost impenetrable black. Its threat most of all: because every shelving projection seemed to hang poised directly above my head; because on every shelf rested precarious fragments of rock that had paused there on an inevitable downward path; and, most vividly of all, because I had to pick my way forward through rubble that had presumably fallen from the cliff face in the half-stutter of geologic time since the last Colorado flood swept like a liquid broom across the submerged slabs." [14]

Riding the River

THE COLORADO RIVER—one of the most treacherous waterways in the United States—is the highlight of the canyon experience for about 22,000 visitors. As "river rat" and former Sierra Club Director Martin Litton wrote in 1977, passengers on a river run

"...will sleep on the ground, and in the days between they will drift through gorges no artist could ever depict and crash through cataracts no open-water sailor would ever believe. When they feel like it, they will explore ashore, up the side canyons to secret springs and gardens and to the ancient buildings where vanished races dwelt a thousand years ago. They will watch the bighorn's leaping ascent of the cliffs, the eagle's soaring flight along the rimrock. They will get to know the beavers, ravens, ouzels, wood rats, lizards, and cacomistles that have never learned to fear humans because they have never had to." [15]

Up to 1909 groups had gone by boat down the full length of the Canyon only six times, all of those runs related to geological or navigational surveys or prospecting. The seventh run of the river, however, was accomplished by industrialist Julius Stone, largely for the fun of it, but also to dispel popular ignorance about the beautiful river. An Ohio native, Stone had come to Glen Canyon to run a gold-dredging operation; though that enterprise failed, a lifelong interest in Grand Canyon river running was begun. To ensure documentation and subsequent publicity he hired a d a newspaperman (for whom a rapid —ned—Dubendorff fell into his rapid, n it). Stone's old friend Nathaniel T. —rst ran the river in 1897, was guide. —was a boon for tourists. During 1911 —b brothers floated down the canyon —camera to create the film that hun— —s of tourists would view for the next —rth also wrote a book about their —olbs actually spent more than one —the Green and Colorado rivers in —amps.

—n, a young man frustrated by his —a crew member spot for organized —the first full solo run on the river in —his own design. He used Ellsworth —navigational reference, and packed —flour, beans, raisins, prunes, bacon, —oods, and minimal equipment. —was all the more remarkable because —the wood boats had usually been —ed by ropes through major rapids.

These techniques de- manded teamwork, but Buzz was alone. Ulti- mately his own exhaus- tion led him to take risks in running supposedly unrunnable rapids—and to live to tell about them!

After the trip, al- though Buzz avoided many of the offers for his story or proposals for other ventures, he was successfully petitioned by Amos Burg, a mem- ber of the New York Ex-

—r man had money to finance a run —perienced canoer with an idea for —was discussing with the Goodyear —When Buzz unexpectedly came —ft from Julius Stone, he and Burg —n, two-boat trip in 1938. On this —came the first man to run every —; and the future was opened for —materials.

—s eclipsed by the first truly com- —nted trip through the canyon, —at very same year. It was led by —boatman who had spent time —uan River. Two women, Elzada —r of Botany at the University of —sistant, Lois Jotter, were among —rofessor, in fact, was instrumen— —e trip. They rode in wooden —gned and named by Nevills. The —uccessful, and the tourist indus— —Nevills himself led so many trips —949, when still only one hundred —anyon, fully one-third of them —n.

Various other firsts took place over the next de- cade. In 1941 the first complete kayak run was made by Alexander Grant. The first powerboat went suc- cessfully downriver in 1949, and in 1951 the first outboard motorboats ran it. But the big news for the tourist trade came in 1954 when a Sierra Club mem- ber named "Georgie" White Clark, who'd been run- ning the canyon in various fashions since the mid 1940s and who became the first woman to handle oars all the way down the canyon in 1952, lashed three inflated surplus army assault rafts together (called "G- rigs" in her honor) and pioneered the large-scale river trips with her "share the expense" company.

John McPhee, a chronicler of man and nature, described Upset Rapid, a typical experience on a commercial river run:

> "With a deep shudder we dropped into a percentage of the hole—God only knows if it was ten—and the raft folded almost in two. The bow and the stern became the high points of a deep V. Water smashed down on us. And down it smashed again, all in that other world of slow and disparate motion. It was not speed but weight that we were experiencing: The great, almost impon- derable, weight of water, enough to crush a thousand people but not hurting us at all because we were part of it—part of the weight, the raft, and the river. Then, surfacing over the far edge of the hole, we bobbed past the incisor rock and through the foaming outwash."[16]

By mid-1954 the second hundred people had run through the canyon. By the end of the decade another three hundred had gone through. The last big chal- lenge to the river rats was the upriver canyon run, which had been attempted repeatedly, starting with the pessimistic Lieutenant Ives. The feat was finally accomplished in 1960, using turbocrafts with marine motors and jet-propulsion units; Otis R. "Dock" Marston, a famous river rat and river historian, was the expedition's navigator.

Running the Grand Canyon is exhilarating. Don't be fooled by the numbers of people who do it—it is still a wild experience. When you run with a commer- cial company you sign waivers acknowledging the potential danger to life and limb (although river guides will tell you that most injuries occur on hikes). Rapids in the canyon are rated on a scale of one to ten, the latter being the most difficult. Other rivers have been scaled to five, but more options are needed for the Colorado to differentiate the thirty-seven-foot drop of Lava Falls versus Crystal's hydraulic holes and standing waves.

Unfortunately, recent federal governments have taken less heed of Teddy Roosevelt's admonitions to "Keep the Grand Cañon as it is." Since 1964 a dam has buried the first thirty-nine miles of Grand Canyon (the government calls it Glen Canyon) under Lake Powell, which has itself become a tourist mecca for houseboats and motorboats. One effect of the dam on the river is that the beaches that once formed naturally from silt are no longer being formed; existing beaches are being scoured away by the dam's man-made fluctuations in water levels. The water is also much colder than natural, since it comes from the bottom of

the great holding tank of the lake, and fish life has been affected. Finally, many of the Colorado's rapids are far more dangerous at low-water levels. Guides can no longer plan against natural water-level fluctuations and must often take on some of the worst rapids under some of the worst conditions.

Conservationists have never given up the protest against this dam. Other dams which would have buried other parts of the canyon, including that supreme rapid, Lava Falls, were subsequently blocked through the massive lobbying and advertising efforts of the Sierra Club. Ironically, the national campaigns against the dams led not just to calls and letters to Congress, but also to another increase in visitor traffic to the canyon itself.

Being There

WHY DOES ONE GO to the Grand Canyon? If the photographs in this volume don't begin to give you an idea, then consider this:

> "No matter how far you have wandered hitherto, or how many famous gorges and valleys you have seen, this one, the Grand Cañon of the Colorado, will seem as novel to you, as unearthly in the color and grandeur and quantity of its architecture, as if you had found it after death, on some other star; so incomparably lovely and grand and supreme it is above all the other cañons in our fire-moulded, earthquake-shaken, rain-washed, wave- washed, river and glacier sculpted world." [17]

Look at it—a sight bigger than you can compre- hend. It stuns you the way an earthquake stuns you, forcing a complete reevaluation of your concepts of the earth.

Hike into it. Sleep in it. Watch the way the moonlight etches each crevice into a different ancient tale as the night progresses. See how the soft dawn light reveals the layered colors that will be lost in brighter day. Can you imagine the pace of layering over two billion years? Listen to the roar of the—even dammed— powerful Colorado River. It has roared for six million years, creating the canyon just as it does today.

> "But now I had accepted the terrible sweep of geologic time and I had felt, superimposed on the deliberate rhythm of the rocks, the pulse of life and the throb of man. I had glimpsed the way these different arcs of time fitted together, one with the other, interlocking. Above all, I had overcome the fear that lurks somewhere deep in most of us, the fear that comes when somebody first says: "Man is a newcomer on earth," the fear that threatens to overwhelm us when we first look back and down into the huge and horrifying vaults of time that ticked away before man existed. And by overcoming this fear I had freed myself." [18]

This is what you go for: for sights wider and eons longer than you can comprehend; for sounds softer and wilder than you can absorb. They are the views, they are the echoes, of everything.

The lights at Grand Canyon Lodge burn brightly on the darkened North Rim. Photograph by Paul Vucetich.

El Tovar (left) welcomes visitors to the South Rim, as it has since 1905. Photograph by D.T. DeDomenico.

NOTES

1. Joseph C. Ives, *Report upon the Colorado River of the West*. Washington, DC: Government Printing Office, 1861, p. 110.

2. Anonymous, as quoted in Martin, Don and Betty. *The Best of Arizona*. Walnut Creek: Pine Cone Press, 1990, p. 24.

3. Charles Dudley Warner, "The Heart of the Desert," 1891, as quoted in Schullery, Paul, ed., *The Grand Canyon: Early Impres- sions*. Boulder: Pruett Publishing Co., 1989, p. 36–40.

4. Harriet Monroe, "The Grand Canyon of the Colorado," 1899, as quoted in Schullery, p. 49.

5. John Muir, "Our Grand Canyon," 1902, as quoted in Schullery, p. 72.

6. Winfield Hogaboom, "To the Grand Canyon in an Automobile," 1902, as quoted in Schullery, p. 63.

7. Irvin Cobb, "Roughing it Deluxe," 1913, as quoted in Schullery, p. 140. Cobb was a writer-humorist for the *Saturday Evening Post*.

8. Ibid, p. 155-156.

9. John Muir, "Our Grand Canyon," 1902, as quoted in Schullery, p. 79.

10. Ibid, p. 84–85

11. John McCutcheon, "Doing the Grand Canyon," 1909, as quoted in Schullery, p. 116.

12. John McCutcheon, "Doing the Grand Canyon," 1909, as quoted in Schullery, p. 120.

13. Colin Fletcher, *The Man Who Walked Through Time*. New York: Alfred A. Knopf, Inc., 1967, p. 5.

14. Ibid, p. 151.

15. Martin Litton, Introduction to John Blaustein, *The Hidden Can- yon: A River Journey*. New York: Penguin Books, 1977, p. 14–15.

16. John McPhee, *Encounters with the Archdruid*. New York: Farrar, Straus & Giroux, 1971, p. 231.

17. John Muir, *Our National Parks*. University of Wisconsin Press, 1901, reprint 1981.

18. Fletcher 1967, p. 211.

Since 1972 LANDSAT has captured d
infrared, which is color coded to corre
or heat radiation. Growing vegetation
areas are blue; deep water is black and
shades of blue. This composite photog
half of Grand Canyon National Park. C
Space Administration.

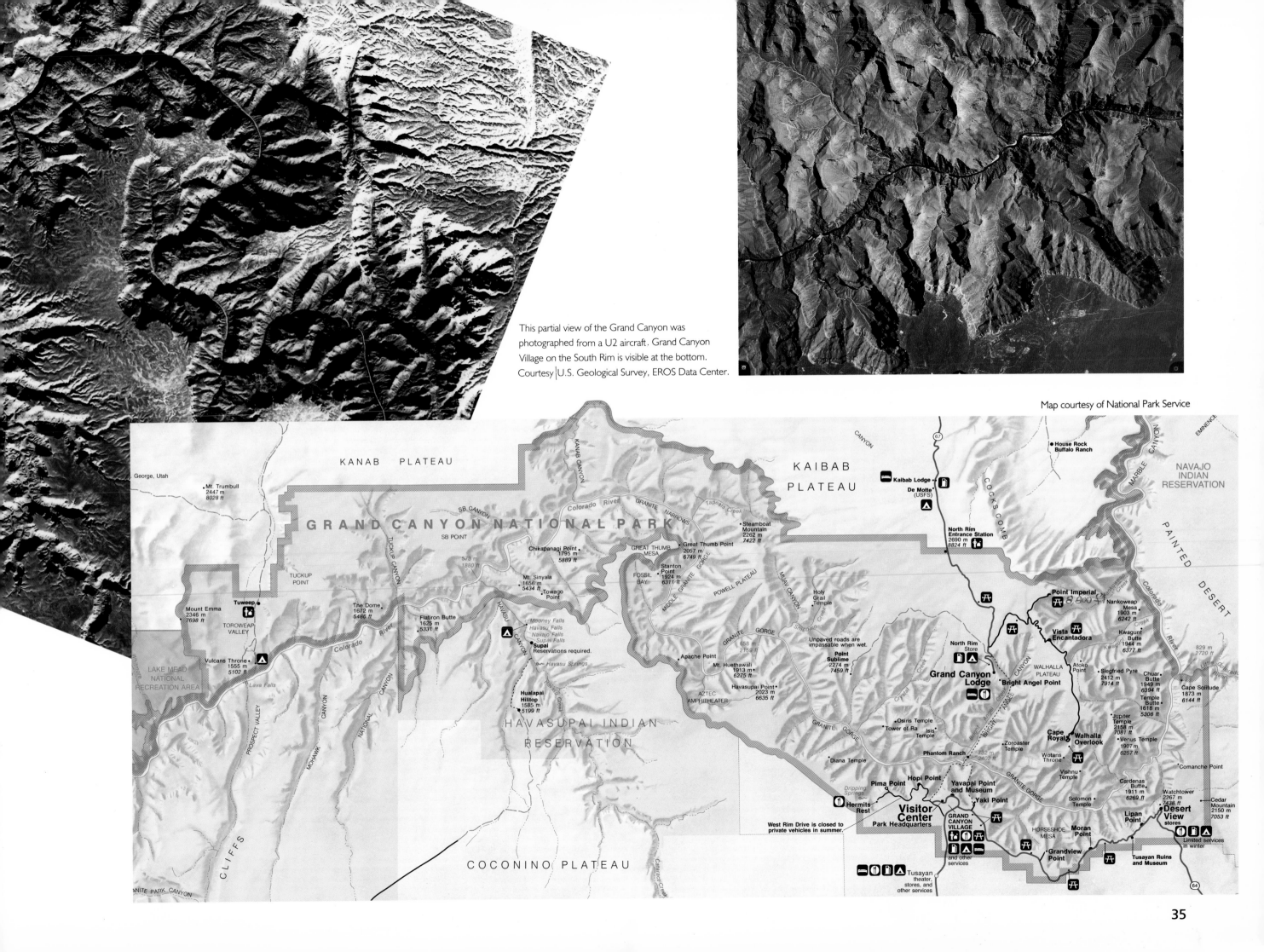

This partial view of the Grand Canyon was photographed from a U2 aircraft. Grand Canyon Village on the South Rim is visible at the bottom. Courtesy U.S. Geological Survey, EROS Data Center.

Map courtesy of National Park Service

KANAB PLATEAU

KAIBAB PLATEAU

House Rock
Buffalo Ranch

Kaibab Lodge
De Motte
(USFS)

St. George, Utah

Mt. Trumbull
2447 m
8028 ft

North Rim
Entrance Station
2690 m
8824 ft

GRAND CANYON NATIONAL PARK

Colorado River

GRANITE NARROWS

Tapeats Creek

SB CANYON

SB POINT

Steamboat
Mountain
2262 m
7422 ft

TUCKUP
POINT

Chikapanagi Point
1795 m
5889 ft

GREAT THUMB
MESA

Great Thumb Point
2057 m
6749 ft

POWELL PLATEAU

Point Imperial
8800 ft

Nankoweap
Mesa
1903 m
6242 ft

Mt. Sinyala
1656 m
5434 m

Towago
Point

Stanton
Point
1924 m
6311 ft

FOSSIL
BAY

Holy
Grail
Temple

NAVAJO
INDIAN
RESERVATION

Vista
Encantadora

Kwagunt
Butte
1944 m
6377 ft

Mount Emma
2346 m
7698 ft

Tuweep

The Dome
1672 m
5486 ft

Flatiron Butte
1625 m
5331 ft

Mooney Falls
Havasu Falls
Navajo Falls
Supai Falls
Reservations required.

GRANITE
GORGE

658 m
2150 ft

Unpaved roads are
impassable when wet.

Point
Sublime
2274 m
7459 ft

North Rim
Store

829 m
2720 ft

Siegfried Pyre
2412 m
7914 ft

Chuar
Butte
1949 m
6394 ft

Temple
Butte
1618 m
5308 ft

Cape Solitude
1873 m
6144 ft

TOROWEAP
VALLEY

Vulcans Throne
1555 m
5102 ft

Colorado
River

Havasu Springs

Apache Point

Mt. Huethawali
1913 m
6275 ft

AZTEC
AMPHITHEATER

Havasupai Point
2023 m
6635 ft

Grand Canyon
Lodge

Bright Angel Point

WALHALLA
PLATEAU

Atoko
Point

Jupiter
Temple
2158 m
7081 ft

Venus Temple
1907 m
6257 ft

LAKE MEAD
NATIONAL
RECREATION AREA

Lava Falls

Hualapai
Hilltop
1585 m
5199 ft

Osiris Temple
Tower of Ra
Isis
Temple

Zoroaster
Temple

Cape
Royal

Walhalla
Overlook

Cardenas
Butte
1911 m
6269 ft

Comanche Point

Watchtower
2267 m
7438 ft

Cedar
Mountain
2150 m
7053 ft

HAVASUPAI INDIAN
RESERVATION

Diana Temple

Phantom Ranch

732 m
2400 ft

Vishnu
Temple

Wotans
Throne

Solomon
Temple

Dripping
Spring

Pima Point

Hopi Point

Yavapai Point
and Museum

Yaki Point

Lipan
Point

Desert
View
stores

CLIFFS

Hermits
Rest

West Rim Drive is closed to
private vehicles in summer.

Visitor
Center
Park Headquarters

GRAND
CANYON
VILLAGE

and other
services

HORSESHOE
MESA

Moran
Point

Grandview
Point

Tusayan Ruins
and Museum

Limited services
in winter

COCONINO PLATEAU

Tusayan
theater,
stores,
and other services

GRANITE PARK CANYON

Cataract Creek

35

Hiking up above Deer Creek, located at about the halfway point on the river journey, affords a panoramic view.

Aerial view of Marble Canyon. Major Powell named Marble Canyon for the Redwall Limestone that is its most distinctive feature, but the term is a misnomer since there is no marble in any of the canyon formations. The confluence of the Little Colorado and Colorado rivers at Mile 61.4 separates Marble Canyon from the Grand Canyon.

The Colorado River cuts a north-south path through Marble Canyon, as seen in this view from Cape Solitude on the South Rim of Grand Canyon National Park.

Moonrise over the North Rim forest

OPPOSITE

Summer lightening storms are common at the Grand
Canyon. Several bolts illuminate the view from Point Imperial
on the North Rim. At 8,800 feet, Point Imperial is the highest
vantage point along the canyon rim.

The vista from Toroweap Overlook has been a favorite of photographers from Jack Hillers to the present day. Located in the ecologically different western sector of the Grand Canyon, Toroweap stands 2,700 feet above the river. From this vantage point Lava Falls, a remnant of volcanic activity that took place one million years ago and still constitutes the most treacherous passage on the river, appears to be a small ripple.

Toroweap Overlook, northwest view

William Henry Holmes, "The Grand Cañon at the Foot of the Toroweap, Looking East," *Tertiary History of the Grand Cañon District, with Atlas.*

"This place exerts a magnetic spell. The sky is there above it, but not of it. Its being is apart; its climate, its light, its own. The beams of sun come into it like visitors. Its own winds blow through it, not those of outside, where we live. The River streams down its mysterious reaches, hurrying ceaselessly; sometimes a smooth sliding lap, sometimes a falling, broken wilderness of billows and whirlpools. Above stand its walls, rising through space upon space of silence. They glow, they gloom, they shine. Bend after bend they reveal themselves, endlessly new in endlessly changing veils of colour. A swimming and jewelled blue predominates, as of saffires being melted and spun into skeins of shifting cobweb. Bend after bend this trance of beauty and awe goes on, terrible as the Day of Judgment, sublime as the Psalms of David. Five thousand feet below the opens and barrens of Arizona, this canyon seems like an avenue conducting to the secret of the universe and the presence of the gods."

OWEN WISTER, foreword to E.L. Kolb, *Through the Grand Canyon from Wyoming to Mexico.*

< Toroweap Overlook, east view at sunrise

41

"Each wall of the canyon is a composite structure, a wall composed of many walls but never a repetition. Every one of these almost innumerable gorges is a world of beauty in itself. In the Grand Canyon these are thousands of gorges like that below Niagara Falls, and there are a thousand Yosemites. Yet all these canyons unite to form one grand canyon, the most sublime spectacle on earth."

JOHN WESLEY POWELL, *Down the Colorado*, 1969.

Confucius Temple viewed from Point Sublime, the terminus of one of the longest promontories into the canyon, which affords a 270-degree view.

OPPOSITE

View to west at sunrise from Point Sublime, North Rim.

Cliffs of Kaibab limestone are stained red by sunrise light at Point Imperial.

Opposite

On a late summer evening, the tops of some formations off Bright Angel Point glow in the last light, but the depths of the canyon are already blanketed in shadow.

5:28 A.M.

7:16 A.M.

12:23 P.M.

Time sequence shot on June 12, 1990, view to the east
from near Mather Point on the South Rim, Grand Canyon
National Park.

Clarence Dutton, a geologist whose survey of the Grand Canyon was published in 1882, noted eloquently the temporal
effects of changing light on the canyon's structures:

"It is never the same. even from day to day, or even from hour to hour. In the early morning its mood and subjective
influences are usually calmer and more full of repose than at other times, but as the sun rises higher the whole scene is so
changed that we cannot recall our first impressions. Every passing cloud, every change in the position of the sun, recasts the
whole. At sunset the pageant closes amid splendors that seem more than earthly. The direction of the full sunlight, the
massing of the shadows, the manner in which the side lights are thrown from the clouds determine these modulations, and
the sensitiveness of the picture to the slightest variations of these conditions is very wonderful."

Tertiary History of the Grand Cañon District, with Atlas.

:19 P.M.

7:07 P.M.

Late afternoon light illuminates a sheer wall of Kaibab limestone, western

view from the porch of Grand Canyon Lodge, North Rim.

The easily identified form of Angel's Window at Cape Royal on the North Rim frames a glimpse of the canyon and supports an unusual vantage point popular with tourists.

OPPOSITE LEFT

Gathering clouds begin to fill a summer sky over Point Imperial; by evening they will bring rain to the canyon.

OPPOSITE RIGHT

Wotans Throne is a distinctive landmark visible from both rims. From the close-up view at Cape Royal, it is possible to imagine the evolution of this fragile, sheer-faced wall of limestone.

OVERLEAF >

Boulders of lava, sandstone, limestone, and conglomerate stone have come

to a temporary rest on the gravel bar at Whitmore Wash at the western

edge of the Grand Canyon. Their presence is evidence of the processes of

weathering, erosion, and transport that continue to sculpt the canyon

Fluted limestone

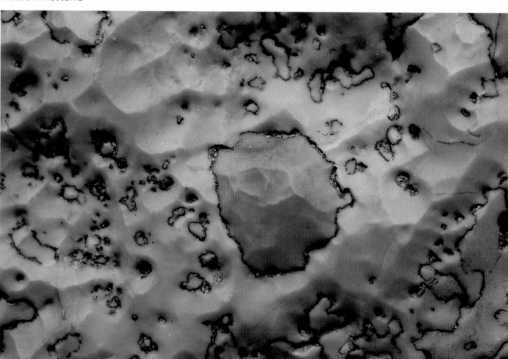

Coral inclusion in creamy white stone

V Sculptural forms in schis

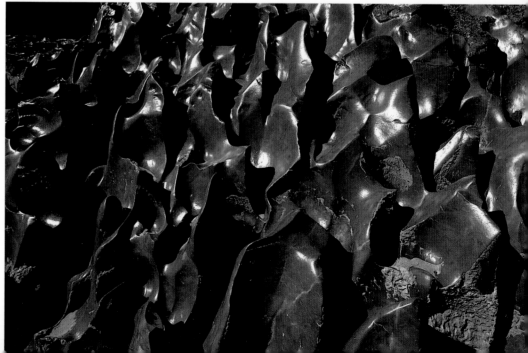

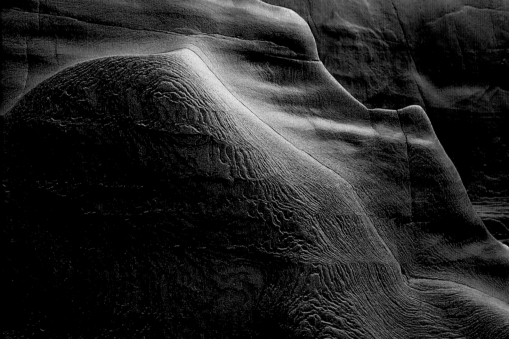
The undulating form of this stone suggests that it was sculpted by water.

Watered rocks at river's edge

Tapeats sandstone   V Supai sandstone

Vishnu Schist   V Limestone at river level with horizontal erosion

Shell fossil and lichen in Kaibab limestone   V Polished ridges in Grand Canyon limestone

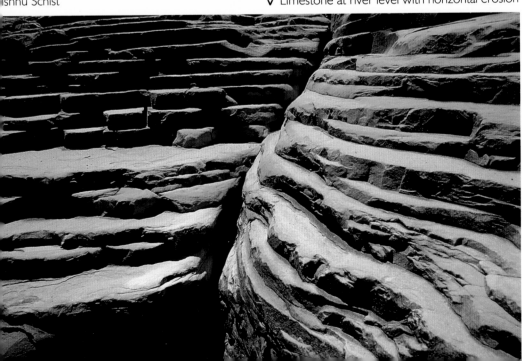
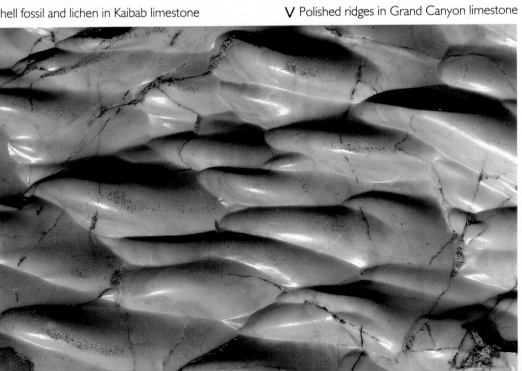

Sunrise light on canyon walls viewed from Horseshoe Mesa

The rising sun warms the layered vista seen from Point Imperial. >

A flock of wild turkeys in a North Rim meadow called The Basin.

Golden leaves of quaking aspen, so called because their leaves flutter in the slightest breeze, contrast green spires of spruce.

Opposite >

Fall foliage brightens a canyon overlook along the Transept Trail of the North Rim.

< Late autumn view above Crystal Creek Canyon, North Rim.

Fallen leaves form a mottled golden carpet beneath the twisted white trucks of aspen trees, North Rim.

Twisted trunks of trees suggest a spirited dance animates a North Rim aspen forest.

The spring green color of budding leaves contrasts white aspen trunks and a late > season snowfall—to which the North Rim is prone because of its altitude.

The subalpine environment of the North Rim hosts a riotous display of wildflowers each spring when the snows melt.

1. Cumulus clouds surmount a field of wildflowers on the North Rim.

2. Butterfly on yarrow flower

3. Watercress (*Rorippa nasturium aquaticum*) is an edible wildflower that delights hikers foraging to supplement their supper.

4. Blue lupine and red Indian Paintbrush are the dominant colors in a field of wildflowers.

5. Skyrocket gilia

6. Monkey flower is typically red, but the yellow variety is found in Grand Canyon.

7. Raindrops on lupine leaves

8. Sego lily

9. Ranunculus

10. Wild form of penstemon

OVERLEAF

At lower altitudes, the canyon environment is hotter and drier, supporting hearty desert flora.

1. Barrel cactus along river embankment

2. Utah juniper

3. Flowers of prickly pear cactus

4. The sacred datura is reputed to be hallucinogenic, but ingesting even a small amount is toxic to humans.

5. Yucca, detail

6. Spring flowers along Cardenas Creek

7. Beaver tail cactus along South Kaibab Trail

1

2

3

1

2

3
4

Evening light on Wotans Throne and Vishnu Temple

Rainstorm after sunset from Yaki Point.

"The Grand Canyon is quintessential canyon country. The bones of the land here lay bare. White ribs of Kaibab Limestone and Coconino Sandstone shine through the distance's softening haze. The dynamic balance between the uplift of the mountains and the downcutting of erosion has momentarily been frozen in the walls of the Canyon. Geology as cinema: running slowly enough that we can examine time frame by frame."

Michael Collier, *An Introduction to Grand Canyon Geology.*

Showers over Marble Canyon.

West rim of Marble Canyon seen from the air.

"For nearly a century the Grand Canyon has been known from its rim. The magnificence of the view from the topmost sharp-edged cliff down to the terraced interior is world famous. The awesome ambiguity of scale fascinates or repels those who gaze into the canyon for the first time. The torn inverted landscape lying spread below is a raw wound in the earth's skin in which the exposed anatomy has the colors of torn flesh. One looks down on buttes, the size of many an eastern mountain, that rise from plains thousands of feet below, though they appear to be within arm's reach. Distances to far cliffs and towers that fade into the indistinct purple haze are measureless. The river, glimpsed in places, seems to be directly below one's feet. So tiny it appears, no bigger than a mountain brook, that the first reaction is incredulity: Can this stream indeed have carved the whole vast landscape? That it is indeed the architect becomes more convincing as one descends and begins to hear and see the river's power."

ELIOT PORTER, *Through the Grand Canyon*, 1969.

< The majestic form of Vishnu Temple in the eastern sector of Grand Canyon.

OVERLEAF

The strong north-south delineation of Bright Angel Canyon, seen from Mather Point on the South Rim, is not obscured by snowfall.

Yavapai Point, one-half mile northeast of the Visitor Center on the South Rim, is one of the most accessible vista points at the Grand Canyon, so its 180-degree view dominates most recollections of canyon formations.

Morning light illuminates a view toward Bright Angel Point,

shot just west of Grand Canyon Village.

Snow-encrusted pinyon pines near Yaki Point

Snow covers the distant palisades seen from

Maricopa Point along West Rim Drive. >

George M. Wheeler prophecized in his 1882 survey,

"These stupendous specimens of extended rock-carvings that make up the system of canyons...stand without rival upon the face of the globe, must always remain one of its wonders, and will, as circumstances of transportation permit, attract the denizens of all quarters of the world who in their travels delight to gaze upon the intricacies of nature."

Grand Canyon Lodge, designed by Gilbert Stanley Underwood who also built the Ahwahnee Hotel at Yosemite, seems to emerge from a ledge of Kaibab limestone on the North Rim.

The crowds and precipitous drops have made it necessary to install barriers at many overlooks along West Rim Drive.

OPPOSITE

A rainbow sparks the sunset view enjoyed by onlookers at Yaki Point on the South Rim of Grand Canyon.

Clouds create a dramatic sky at sunset, viewed from an
observation deck near Grand Canyon Lodge, North Rim.

A double rainbow arches over the river corridor, Grand Canyon.

Limestone ledges near Moran Point on the South Rim. >

A morning storm at Desert View casts an eerie glow over the forces of erosion that constitute the canyon.

< Opposite Left

Rainbow over the North Rim

< Top

Cumulo nimbus clouds gather and deposit rain over the Little Colorado River.

< Bottom

The canyon, viewed from Grand Canyon Lodge with Angel's Gate at center, fills with fog at dusk.

79

Heavy snow on the rim and fog in the canyon
mark a winter day.

Opposite>

Photographer Greg Probst used to walk through this
Ponderosa pine forest on South Rim every day on his way to
work, so on President's Day, 1990, when he saw new-fallen
snow, he had mentally composed the desired shot. Old-
growth Ponderosa pine is called "pumpkin pine" for the
coloration of its bark.

Sunrise illuminates a wintery canyon scene from Mather Point.

Opposite

Winter fog obscures a similar view from Mather Point. The structure in left foreground is also seen in a similar position in photo at left. Two distinctive forms at the center of each picture are Wotans Throne (flat-top pyramid) and Vishnu Temple (pyramid surmounted by triangular form).

Overleaf

The astounding range of colors in canyon formations is visible from Yaki Point.

At sunset tourists are silhouetted against the flaming sky at Powell Point overlook.

Visitors enjoy the view from Powell Point, named in honor>

of Major John Wesley Powell who first navigated and surveyed the Grand Canyon.

"*Stand at some point on the brink of the Grand Canyon where you can overlook the river, and the details of the structure, the vast labyrinth of gorges of which it is composed, are scarecely noticed; the elements are lost in the grand effect, and a broad, deep flaring gorge of many colors is seen. But stand down among these gorges and the landscape seems to be composed of huge vertical elements of wonderful form. Above, it is an open, sunny gorge; below, it is deep and gloomy. Above, it is a chasm; below, it is a stairway from gloom to heaven.*"
JOHN WESLEY POWELL, *Down the Colorado*, 1969.

An aerial view of Chuar Butte, which is the dominant landmark at the intersection of the Colorado and Little Colorado rivers, is also visible from various spots on the rim.

OPPOSITE

The view to the north and west from Lipan Point includes the silhouette of Chuar Butte, which rises on the left bank of the river at the northernmost point where the water is visible from the rim.

Mule trains are a popular alternative to hiking the South Kaibab Trail.

OPPOSITE

Panoramic views can be seen from the back of a mule, a form of transportation as old as tourism at the Canyon.

The blacksmith, a craftsman who has disappeared from most of America, is still keep busy shoeing the popular mule trains at the Grand Canyon. Mitch De Ville, who recently joined the South Rim stables, controls an ornery mule with an elaborate harness.

OVERLEAF

Panorama of Kaibab Trail with hikers.

INSET

Cedar Ridge, 1.5 miles from the head of the South Kaibab Trail, affords panoramic views to those who make the pleasant hike. The return trip to the rim takes twice as long as the descent, so hikers should allow enough time and be well provisioned with water.

<Bright Angel Trail zigzags to the river.

The Kaibab Suspension Bridge crosses the Colorado near the mouth of Bright Angel Creek. Its 440-foot span is elevated 60 feet above the river to prevent its being washed out in a flood, the fate of an earlier structure crossing the river.

LEFT

Phantom Ranch, which harbors overnight guests with advance reservations, is a welcome sight to tired hikers.

National Park Service patrol boats beached along the Colorado River.

Navajo Falls at Supai

Thunder River is fed by a spring at the base of the Redwall

formation, then cascades down a sheer cliff to Tapeats Creek.

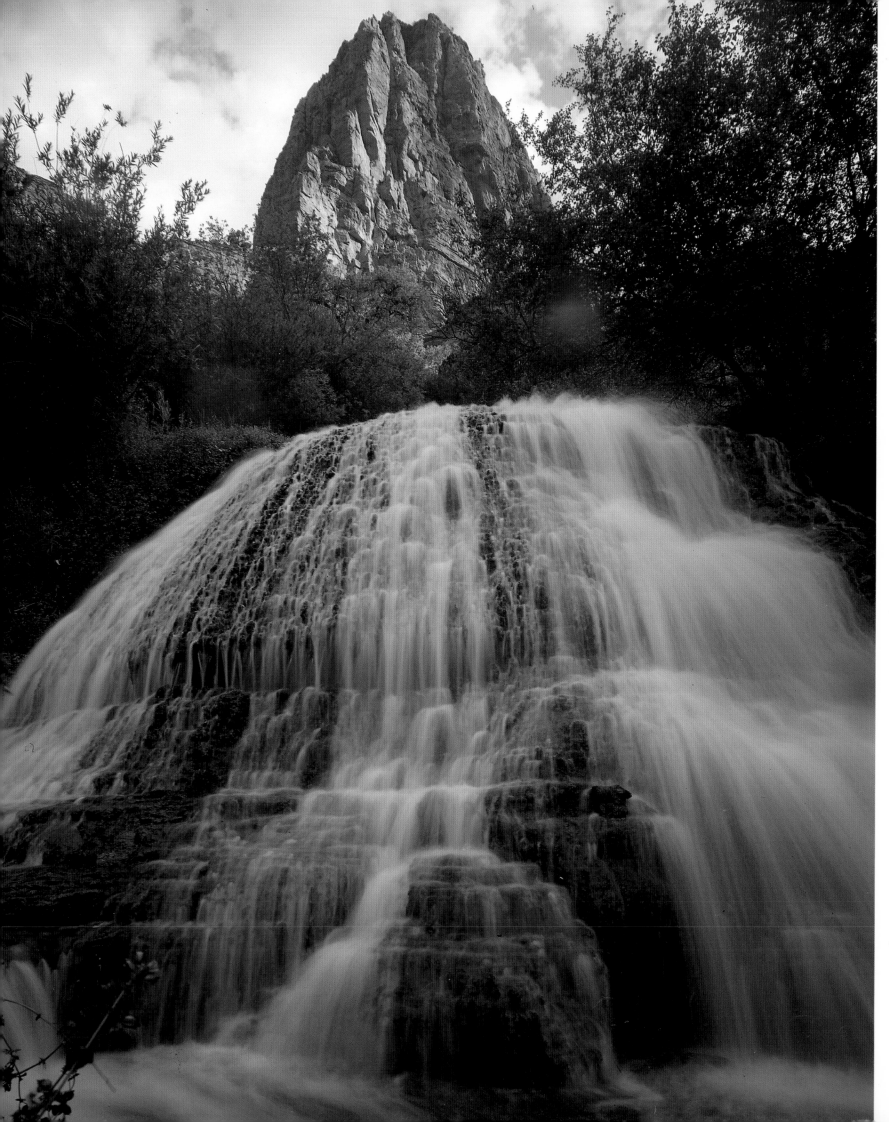

< The sound of Roaring Springs is quite audible from Bright Angel Point, although they are located 3,500 feet below the rim. Water has been pumped from Roaring Springs to supply the North Rim since 1928.

Chevaya Falls, the largest (600 ft) waterfall in Grand Canyon runs only during spring melt off.

97

Looking downriver from President Harding Rapid, Mile 44
on river journey through Grand Canyon.

RIGHT
Tapeats Creek (on left) joins the Colorado River (on right).
Building storm and setting sun provide contrasting lighting.

"Between the cataracts, the stream outspreads to great width and rushes swiftly by. It is almost always turbid, and generally is charged with a heavy load of sand and silt. On the lowest talus near the brink may be seen lines of the high-water mark, some as high as fifty or sixty feet above the ordinary summer stages. Within those stages the rocks are ground and polished, carved into strange shapes, and worn by potholes from the scouring of the current. All of the boulders are rounded and ground away, or have become carious and crumbly by the chemical reactions of air and water. All things plainly reveal the powerful effects of corrosion acting with extreme energy. We do not wonder at it now. The impetuous rush of the waters charged with sharp sand even at lower stages is amply suggestive, and the mind is at a loss to conceive what must be the power of the river when its volume is many times multiplied."

CLARENCE E. DUTTON, *Tertiary History of the Grand Cañon District, with Atlas*, 1882.

Menacing sky threatens the Grand Canyon with more rain, >
but the color of the Colorado—which means "red-colored"—
suggests that much loose soil has been transported into the
river by recent storms.

To reach this pool carved into the ancient Supai formation, one must hike a mile into North Canyon from near Mile 20 on the river.

Human figures are dwarfed by the swooping vault of Redwall Cavern.

OPPOSITE

Redwall Cavern, a wide-mouthed cave carved into Marble Canyon at Mile 33, was described by Major Powell as "a vast half-circular chamber which, if utilized for a theatre, would give seating to 50,000."

"At another place there were hundreds of carvings on a similar wall which overhung a little. Drawings of mountain sheep were plentiful; there was one representing a human figure with a bow and arrow, and with a sheep standing on the arrow—their way of telling that he got the sheep, no doubt. There were some masked figures engaged in a dance, not unlike some of the Hopi dances of today, as they picture them. There were geometrical figures, and designs of many varieties."

E.L. KOLB, *Through the Grand Canyon from Wyoming to Mexico.*

TOP AND BOTTOM RIGHT

The Anasazi granaries at Nankoweap above the Colorado River are the most spectacular ruins of 1,000 sites built by Native American people before A.D. 1300.

OPPOSITE TOP LEFT

A feather offering (paho) at the Hopi salt mines, a site near the confluence of the Little Colorado and Colorado rivers that has been placed off limits to visitors by the National Park Service. The Hopi used to run fifty miles along the so-called Salt Trail to collect salt, a precious commodity in the desert, at this location.

1

2

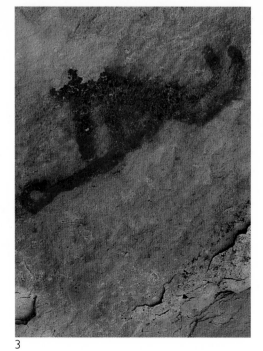

3

4

102

7

8

9

10

Scenic view at Mile 124 of the Colorado River, between Forster and Fossil rapids.

Ripple patterns in low water at Hance Rapid (Mile 77) on the Colorado River.

The acid blue reflection of the sky at Mile 137 of the Colorado River.

At day's end at the western end of the Grand Canyon, the

scene is washed in silver.

Dusk falls quietly on craggy canyon walls,

which have been formed during the past four million

years and record two billion years of geologic activity.

A view of Granite Falls (at Mile 93) from the cliffs above.

William Henry Holmes, "Granite Falls, Kaibab Division," from
Tertiary History of the Grand Cañon District, with Atlas.

Photographer and boatman John Blaustein used a long
exposure to emphasize the white water at Granite Falls, one
of the most treacherous passages on the river journey.

Rafting through a peaceful stretch of Marble Canyon.

"Running the rapids in the Colorado is a series of brief experiences, because the rapids themselves are short. In them, with the raft folding and bending—sudden hills of water filling the immediate skyline—things happen in slow motion. The projector of our own existence slows way down, and you dive as in a dream, and gradually rise, and fall again. The raft shudders across the ridgelines of water cordilleras to crash softly into the valleys beyond. Space and time in there are something other than they are out here....Elapsed stopwatch time has no meaning at all."

JOHN MCPHEE, *Encounters with the Archdruid*, 1971.

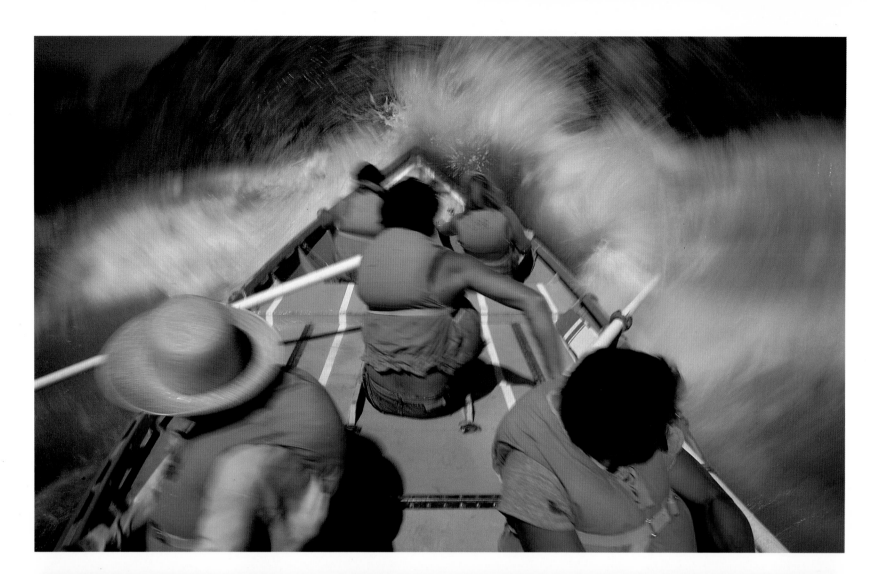

River raft fighting its way through white water.

Kayaking into Deer Creek Falls is an exhilirating experience.

Sunset brings a dramatic end to a summer day on the river:

reflecting on intricate clouds (above): framing the view

downstream from the Anasazi granaries at Nankoweap, Mile

52 (right); in Marble Canyon (opposite).

"Meanwhile, we were enjoying one of those remarkable Arizona desert sunsets. Ominous clouds had been gathering in the afternoon, rising from the southwest, drifting across the canyon, and piling up against the north wall....A yellow flame covered the western sky, to be succeeded in a few minutes by a crimson glow. The sharply defined colours of the different layers of rock had merged and softened, as the sun dropped from sight; purple shadows crept into the cavernous depths, while shafts of gold shot to the very tiptop of the peaks, or threw their shadows like silhouettes on the wall beyond. Then the scene shifted again and it was all blood-red, reflecting from the sky and staining the rocks below, so that distant wall and sky merged, with little to show where the one ended and the other began. That beautiful haze, which tints, but does not obscure, enshrouded the temples and spires, changing from heliotrope to lavender, from lavender to deepest purple; there was a departing flare of flame like the collapse of a burning building; a few clouds in the zenith, torn by the winds so that they resembled the craters of the moon, were tinted for an instant around the rims; the clouds faded to a dove-like gray; they darkened; the gray disappeared; the purple crept from the canyon into the arched dome overhead; the day was ended, twilight passed, and darkness settled over all."

ELLSWORTH KOLB, *Through the Grand Canyon from Wyoming to Mexico.*

OVERLEAF

John Blaustein credits the photographs of Ernst Haas, a passenger in a boat that Blaustein steered through the Grand Canyon in 1972, with inspiring these abstractions of water.

Havasu Creek, a tributary of the Colorado, flows through Havasu Canyon and the village inhabited by the Havasupai people. Havasupai land holdings greatly increased in the 1970s, as part of a congressional decree to enlarge Grand Canyon National Park, and now include traditional grazing lands.

Two views of Havasu Falls. Calcium carbonate in the water gives Havasu Creek its distinctive blue-green color.

Elves Chasm, a landmark at Mile 116 on the river, is another formation created by mineral-laden water percolating through the limestone. It is carpeted by maidenhead fern, columbine, and other thirsty plants found only where water is plentiful in the arid river landscape. Major Powell may have been describing this site in his journal entry of August 23, 1869:

"We pass a stream on the right, which leaps into the Colorado by a direct fall of more than a hundred feet, forming a beautiful cascade. There is a bed of very hard rock above, thirty or forty feet in thickness, and much softer beds below. The hard beds above project many yards beyond the softer, which are washed out, forming a deep cave behind the fall, and the stream pours through a narrow crevice into a deep pool below. Around on the rocks, in the cave-like chamber, are set beautiful ferns, with delicate fronds and enameled stalks....This delicate foliage covers the rocks all about the fountain, and gives the chamber great beauty. But we have little time to spend in admiration, so on we go."

The seeps support water-loving greenery, not otherwise seen in the rocky canyon.

Right

Mooney Falls on Havasu Creek

Minerals deposited by Ribbon Falls have created a travertine mound at least 60 feet high, hidden in an alcove off a trail through Bright Angel Canyon.

"In Grand Canyon, acquifers in the Redwall limestone feed springs on the canyon sides where the lime-laden waters, on exposure to air, redeposit the dissolved mineral in formations like those that surround hot springs or that occur as stalactites and stalagmites in caves. These accretions, which in time build up into huge mounds of reticulated porous stone called travertine, are found in many places on the lower walls of Grand Canyon."

ELIOT PORTER, *Down the Colorado*, 1969.

119

Bright Angel Creek, Roaring Springs on cliff face.

Deer Creek has carved a narrow gorge in the Tapeats sandstone, then emerges fully as a waterfall.

Deer Creek, spring-fed tributary of the Colorado, merges with the river at Mile 136.

This desert landscape that at first look seems so inhospitable, teems with life, including the animals pictured on the next two spreads.

1. Grey fox surveys the canyon from a rocky perch.

2. Implausibly, this snake swallowed a deer mouse whole.

3. Grand Canyon rattlesnake

4. Snake ascends a steep rock face.

5. Bighorn sheep with lamb. These animals, once rarely seen in the canyon, have become more numerous since the wild burros that preyed on them have been eliminated.

6. Scorpion

7. Baby deer mouse learning to climb.

8. Gila Monster

9. Mule deer (*Odocoileus hemionus*) foraging in field of lupine.

10. Wild burros

OVERLEAF

1. Immature golden eagle

2. Kaibab squirrel is an endangered species found only on the North Rim.

3. In its evolution, this small frog has attained a copper coloration uniquely suited to the riverine environment.

4. Banded gecko

5. Tree lizards, despite their name, do not live in trees but are often found on steep rock faces along the river.

6. Ravens

7. Snowy egrets on red-brown rocks in Marble Canyon

8. Lyrical pattern of lizards on rocks

9. Owl

1

2

3

4

5

6

7

8

9

10

1

2

3

4

5

6

7

8

9

Teddy Roosevelt, on a 1903 visit, enunciated a wish for the canyon that is shared by most visitors:

"In the Grand Canyon, Arizona has a natural wonder which, so far as I know, is in kind absolutely unparalleled throughout the rest of the world. I want to ask you to do one thing in connection with it, in your own interest and in the interest of the country—to keep this great wonder of nature as it is now....The ages have been at work on it and man can only mar it. What you can do is to keep it for your children, your children's children, and for all who come after you, as the one great sight which every American who can travel at all should see."

Last rays of the sun illuminate the distinctive forms of Wotans Throne and Vishnu Temple, as the moon rises.

OPPOSITE

Sunset view from the North Rim, past Deva, Brahma, Zoroaster Temples to South Rim.

OVERLEAF

Moonrise over Redwall limestone.